GANDHI, CEO

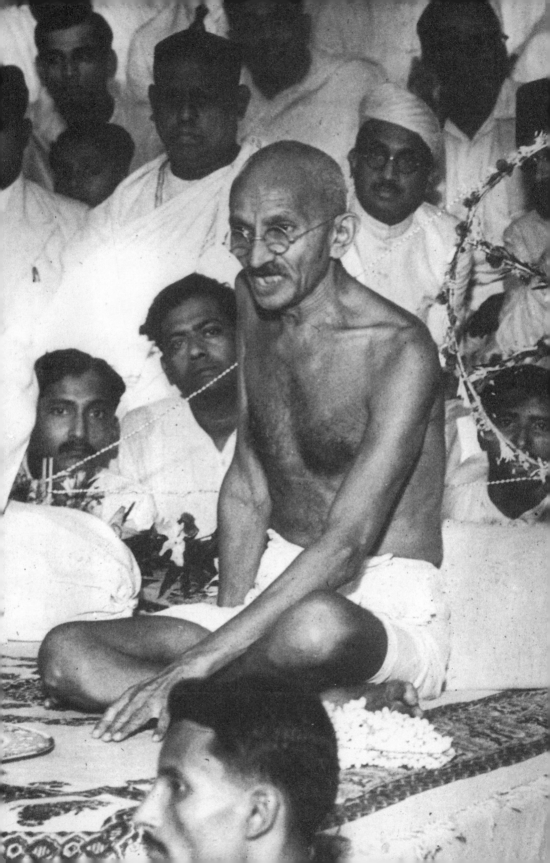

GANDHI, CEO

14 PRINCIPLES TO GUIDE & INSPIRE MODERN LEADERS

ALAN AXELROD

STERLING

New York / London
www.sterlingpublishing.com

STERLING and the distinctive Sterling logo are registered trademarks of
Sterling Publishing Co., Inc.

10 9 8 7 6 5 4 3 2 1

Published by Sterling Publishing Co., Inc.
387 Park Avenue South, New York, NY 10016
© 2010 Sterling Publishing Co., Inc.
Text © 2010 by Alan Axelrod
Distributed in Canada by Sterling Publishing
c/o Canadian Manda Group, 165 Dufferin Street
Toronto, Ontario, Canada M6K 3H6
Distributed in the United Kingdom by GMC Distribution Services
Castle Place, 166 High Street, Lewes, East Sussex, England BN7 1XU
Distributed in Australia by Capricorn Link (Australia) Pty. Ltd.
P.O. Box 704, Windsor, NSW 2756, Australia

Manufactured in the United States
All rights reserved

Sterling ISBN 978-1-4027-5806-5

For information about custom editions, special sales, premium and
corporate purchases, please contact Sterling Special Sales
Department at 800-805-5489 or specialsales@sterlingpublishing.com.

Frontispiece: Mahatma Gandhi tries to settle a Congress Party dispute in Calcutta,
India, in 1934. (Associated Press)

Right: © Shutterstock/Albert Campbell

For Anita and Ian

"Love is the subtlest force in the world."

~ Gandhi

CONTENTS

GANDHI, CEO

14 PRINCIPLES TO GUIDE & INSPIRE MODERN LEADERS

Preface

"Generations to come will scarce believe that such a one as this ever in flesh and blood walked upon this earth."

~Albert Einstein

It is surprisingly easy to believe in the miracles of sainthood, but very hard to believe in those of flesh and blood, the prodigies of leadership that transform the world and the way we see and move and act in the world. Yet, as Gandhi himself taught, these are not miracles at all. They are necessary actions, the works any people, any nation, any enterprise must successfully create, not to achieve the supernatural or merely to survive, but to evolve, to grow, and to prosper.

There is no doubt that Gandhi was a good man and an intensely spiritual man, but he was also a manager and executive, a supremely practical leader for change. Brought up in the Hindu merchant caste, he applied the principles of the Hindu faith and Jain tradition to the challenges of living. He came to believe that truth, tolerance, sacrifice, joy, and the nonviolent rejection of tyranny were not "spiritual" or "visionary" ideals, but the very substance of a successful life that enables, even as it is enabled by, a successful society. Even more, these are the drivers of any worthwhile enterprise, the pragmatic principles which any leader who aspires to sustainable—that is, ethical—success must accept, manage, and master.

But *Gandhi*? A *CEO*?

Consider his achievements: He stimulated and enabled the rebirth of India, at the time a dysfunctional, failing enterprise on which the welfare of millions depended, and he redefined the very medium—civilization, no less—in which that enterprise operated. The means by which Gandhi achieved this included mastering the elements of personal leadership and institutional management, performing a revolutionary analysis of the environment of "business as usual," and formulating a strategy for productively breaking out of the all-too-limiting box of conventional thought, outworn tradition, and received wisdom.

Gandhi embodied what today would be recognized as the "servant leadership" paradigm, which he applied to create an enterprise of utmost efficiency, its objectives and goals sharply defined and rigorously pared down to what matters—and only what matters. For Gandhi, the object was to waste nothing and to reject nothing but untruth, intolerance, and violence. Yet his inclusive approach was focused with laser-like intensity on the essentials, the goals that had to be achieved (as he put it) on a "do or die" basis. For, ultimately, it is only the do-or-die goals that are worth achieving.

They can never be achieved by coercion. For this reason, Gandhi had to become a virtuoso in the art of persuasion through suasion, continually revealing sacrifice as self-interest, the most powerful motivator of all. The result was a nearly ideal organization that achieved the nearly impossible. And it is our good fortune that the master wrote extensively and with great clarity about his assumptions, his principles, his objectives, his experience, and, above all, his methods, inviting us to learn them and to apply them to any worthwhile collaborative endeavor, no matter how humble or how great.

■

The history of India can be traced back some nine thousand years, and the history of British India to the early seventeenth century, although the British Raj—the period of colonial rule—did not begin until 1858. A movement for Indian home rule was gathering momentum by the 1880s, and, beginning in the early twentieth century, largely under the leadership of Gandhi, the home rule movement metamorphosed into a drive for full independence. Amid all of this, the rich complexity of Indian culture—especially the multiplicity of its religions—was and remains, to most Westerners, dazzling if not bewildering. Even the events that were concentrated during the span of Gandhi's own active career are remote and unfamiliar to us. As for Gandhi himself, although he was a tireless campaigner who literally walked the length and breadth of the Indian subcontinent, he was an astoundingly prolific author and letter writer, the modern edition of his complete works running to one hundred volumes.

To adequately study the life and work of Mohandas Gandhi requires, as it merits, the work of a lifetime. Yet anyone can profit from even a fragmentary acquaintance with his experience and thought. *Gandhi, CEO* offers an accessible approach between the comprehensive and the fragmentary. From Gandhi's life's work as a leader of change, one hundred "lessons" have been distilled here into principles designed to inspire and guide the modern and aspiring CEO, manager, or supervisor in building and leading an ethical and profitable enterprise.

■

Ethical and profitable. There was a time—and not too long ago—when business leaders, if they were being brutally honest with themselves, would have hesitated to utter these two adjectives in the same breath. The most cynical among them believed the two words expressed virtually incompatible attributes of a business, but even the more idealistic CEOs and managers tended to think that ethics were a desirable adjunct to profits—valuable, to be sure, but an *added* value, decidedly peripheral, something in the way of a bonus.

That time is over. The world's economic experience in the first decade of the twenty-first century has demonstrated that, far from being optional in business, let alone incompatible with profit, sound ethics are integral with the processes of commerce and are essential to sustained profitability. Gandhi could have told any businessperson this very thing a hundred years ago, during the first decade of the twentieth century. In this book, he tells us now.

Introduction

A Life

Mohandas Karamchand Gandhi was born on October 2, 1869, in the coastal town of Porbandar, now a part of Gujarat, which borders Pakistan to the northwest and the Indian state of Rajasthan to the north and northeast. He was the youngest child of Hindu parents—Karamchand and Putlibai—who were members of the Modh Bania subcaste of Vaishya, the caste of merchants and dairy farmers. The Gandhis had originally been grocers, but both Karamchand and his father served as diwans of Porbandar state—essentially ministers who attended to certain affairs of state and acted as liaisons between the prince and the British government's chief administrative officer, called the political agent. For the most part, it was a comfortable existence, except when internecine violence periodically broke out within the administration of Porbandar state. On one occasion state soldiers laid siege to the Gandhi house; in a separate incident Karamchand was placed under arrest. Despite such minor civil convulsions, he not only survived and persevered in office but emerged as a highly popular political figure who served in the Rajasthanik Court, a government agency charged with arbitrating disputes among colonial India's many states—numbering about three hundred during the late nineteenth century.

Mohandas Gandhi greatly admired his father, whose practical political wisdom, skill in resolving conflicts, and personal courage served as his earliest examples of social leadership. What especially impressed young Gandhi was the way in which his father built a political career dedicated to selfless service and based not on a foundation of formal education—he had had little enough of that—but on experience, principled judgment, and a deep sympathy with the needs of those he served. Karamchand Gandhi had little interest in creating personal wealth and left only a small inheritance to his six children.

Mohandas Gandhi's mother, Putlibai, was Karamchand's fourth wife and almost a quarter-century junior to her husband. Like him, she had little formal education, but she was more religious than he, going daily to the *haveli* (Vaishnava temple) and continually making—and keeping—demanding religious vows. Her example of devotion and spiritual willpower would inform Gandhi's mature career, and her reverence for Jainism, one of India's oldest faiths, was a source of Gandhi's commitment to nonviolence as well as his vegetarianism.

Gandhi attended primary school at Porbandar but showed no special flair for his studies and was also painfully shy. His most valuable education as a youngster came not in the classroom but at his father's side, listening to discussions concerning local disputes, problems of the state, and issues of religion. The Gandhi family was popular in the community, and the house was frequently visited by Hindus as well as Muslims.

In 1881, Gandhi enrolled in high school at Rajkot. At last, his academic performance improved, and while he never developed enthusiasm or skill in sports, he did acquire the habit of taking long walks—something that would serve him well in his adult life, most notably the epic 240-mile Salt March of 1930 in defiance of the British salt tax and other oppressive colonial laws. Despite being haunted by morbid fears of thieves, ghosts, and serpents, he shed some of his earlier shyness and enthusiastically embraced the friendship of Sheikh Mehtab, a lusty youth who goaded him into undertaking a number of dubious experiments, including a visit to a brothel (though Gandhi later claimed that he did not have sex there), indulgence in tobacco, and even the commission of a theft. As an adult, Gandhi regretted these transgressions less than his yielding to Mehtab's insistence that he become a meat eater. His friend argued that a vegetarian diet kept Hindus weak, whereas a meat diet gave the British the strength to rule India. Reflecting on his own frail build and what he considered his timid ways, Gandhi let himself be persuaded, and for about a year he sneaked meat into his diet. For years to come, far more disturbing to his conscience than the violation of a religious dietary law was the act of lying to his parents.

In 1883, thirteen-year-old Gandhi was married to Kasturba (later known to Gandhi affectionately as "Ba"), to whom he had been betrothed seven years earlier. Such arranged marriages were traditional in Hindu culture and were motivated less by religious belief than by reasons of economy; parents were eager to get their daughters out from under their roofs. A native of Gujarat, Kasturba was illiterate but possessed a lively mind and a strong, even stubborn, disposition. The couple's early life together was tumultuous, and Gandhi later regretted his quite literally childish efforts to compel Kasturba to conform to his will. The experience not only persuaded him that voluntary obedience alone was a valid form of compliance, but it also prompted Gandhi to become an eloquent opponent of arranged child marriages. Nevertheless, the two grew to mutual devotion, and Kasturba participated in many of Gandhi's campaigns for social change and justice, often subjecting herself to arrest and imprisonment along with her husband.

Two years into the marriage their first child was born, but he lived only a few days. (The Gandhis went on to have four more children, all boys: Harilal, born 1888; Manilal, 1892; Ramdas, 1897;

and Devdas, 1900). The sorrow of this event was compounded by the death of Gandhi's long-ailing father earlier that year. Although young Mohandas had nursed the man faithfully, he was not at his bedside when he died, a fact over which Gandhi felt a lifelong, mingled sense of guilt and regret.

In 1887, Gandhi passed the entrance exam for admission to Samaldas College in Bhavnagar, Gujarat, and was admitted but left after a single term to sail for England, where, against the wishes of some in his family, he intended to study law. Although Modh Bania elders excommunicated him from the caste for his decision to go to England, Gandhi placated his mother with vows to abstain from alcohol, women, and—above all—meat. Leaving son and wife behind, he sailed from Bombay (present-day Mumbai) in September 1888.

Mohandas Gandhi found life in the strange new country difficult at first. His shyness returned with a vengeance, and he struggled mightily to improve his halting English. Craving acceptance in English society, young Gandhi affected the dress and manners of what he conceived to be the perfect "English gentleman." His clothing was expensively tailored, he took both elocution and dancing lessons, and when his attempts at keeping rhythm failed, he took up the violin. As for his vegetarianism, he tried to explain it away to meat-eating English acquaintants as a harmless fad. After some searching, he found a vegetarian restaurant in his area of London and, for the first time in his life, became a vegetarian out of conviction and not just in obedience to religion and parental tradition. Indeed, he made his first London friends—and discovered a talent for organizing people who held unconventional, even radical ideas—when he founded a vegetarian club in his neighborhood of Bayswater. Later, he served on the Executive Committee of the city's Vegetarian Society, but even at this stage of his life, he had yet to acquire the full courage of his convictions and was reticent to speak up at meetings.

Within only a matter of months, Gandhi's uncritical Anglophilia passed. It was not so much that he felt he was being untrue to himself, as that it was an impractical waste of time and money. After all, he did not intend to stay in England, so why become English? Still, removal from his familiar surroundings did have some beneficial effects. It prompted him to reflect on his beliefs objectively, and Gandhi began earnestly studying religion. For the first time in his life, he read the Bhagavad Gita, the New Testament, and works by Theosophist authors, who were in vogue during this time. What struck him was the commonality of certain values across divergent faiths—especially nonviolence and the spiritual benefits of voluntary renunciation. Gandhi was also exposed for the first time in his life to the various secular movements of the modern Western world, especially socialism and anarchism.

Almost incidentally to these eye-opening, life-changing experiences, Gandhi earnestly studied the law and passed the bar examinations. After qualifying as a barrister and enrolling in the High Court in June 1891, he returned to India after a three years absence—only to discover that his London legal training had not really prepared him for a career in Indian law. There was much about Indian legal customs that he did not like, especially the lawyer's practice of paying "touts" to send cases his way. Even worse, Gandhi soon realized that arguing before a judge and other lawyers made him nervous to the point of illness and incoherence. When a request for his services from an Indian firm in South Africa reached him, he was eager for an escape and sailed in April 1893.

■

An escape? The move to South Africa proved fateful, transporting Gandhi to what would become his life's work. The small South African Indian community was the object of persecution by the white majority, who regarded "coolies" (as they derogatorily called Indians) as nothing more or less than a source of cheap labor. When some sought more in life—to own farms and start businesses—they were stifled by restrictive legislation and heavy taxation while also denied the rights of citizens, including the vote. Racial discrimination was institutionalized on every level. In May 1893, while traveling by train from Durban, Natal, to Pretoria, Transvaal, to prosecute a lawsuit for a Muslim client, Gandhi experienced social injustice firsthand. The incident illustrated that, in South Africa, "as a man and as an Indian I had no rights." It was a harsh awakening.

His law firm had booked a first-class train compartment for his trip. When the train stopped at Maritzburg, capital of Natal, a white man boarded, poked his head into Gandhi's compartment, and then withdrew it in obvious disgust. Minutes later, he returned with (as Gandhi recalled) "one or two officials. They all kept quiet, when another official came to me and said, 'Come along, you must go to the van [third-class] compartment.'"

"But I have a first-class ticket," Gandhi protested.

"That doesn't matter," the official replied. "I tell you, you must go to the van compartment."

"I tell you," Gandhi asserted, "I was permitted to travel in this compartment in Durban and I insist on going on in it."

Exasperated, the official spat out an ultimatum to get out "or else I shall have to call a police constable to push you out."

There are moments when a few uttered words change the course of one's life. For Gandhi, this was such a moment.

Without raising his voice, he replied to the ultimatum: "Yes you may. I refuse to get out voluntarily."

It was Mohandas Gandhi's first assertion of nonviolent "passive resistance."

In short order, he was tossed off the train along with his luggage and spent a cold, miserable night in the waiting room of the Maritzburg station. The white men on the now-departed train figured that they had won—and to all appearances, they had—but as Gandhi realized, all they had succeeded in doing was throwing him off a train. They did not—and could not—force him to "get out voluntarily." As he pondered alone in the chilly darkness of the railroad station, three courses seemed open to him: to fight for his rights, to chuck it all and return to India, or to proceed to Pretoria and prosecute the case for which he had been hired.

Rejecting a return to India, he decided first to finish the case—it was his duty, after all—but afterward he resolved to do even more than fight for *his* rights. The indignity offered him was, he believed, "only a symptom of the deep disease of color prejudice." He determined to "try, if possible, to root out the disease and suffer hardships in the process." Seeing his treatment as but a single manifestation of widespread injustice, he vowed to do no less than change South African government and society. He could not know it at the time, but, ridiculously ambitious as this goal was, it fell far short of what he would ultimately attempt: to change the world by leading the minds and the hearts of humankind to the most profound of transformations. Gandhi had boarded the train in Durban a reluctant and not terribly successful barrister. Ejected at Maritzburg, he emerged a reformer of great vision and courage.

■

In Pretoria, Gandhi met with local Indian community leaders and proposed forming an association to win rights for Indians in South Africa. He organized laborers and sympathizers in passive resistance campaigns and founded the Natal Indian Congress to coordinate the movement. In January 1887, a white mob assaulted Gandhi and nearly beat him to death. His response—as typical as it was dramatic—was to forgive his attackers.

In the midst of the struggle for Indian rights, the Second ("Great") Boer War broke out in 1899 between the British colonial government and the Dutch "Boers." Although Gandhi's natural inclination was to side with the Boers, who were mostly hard-scrabble farmers, he believed that, as a citizen of the empire, he owed service to the British. His creed of nonviolence would not permit his taking up arms, but he quickly organized an eleven-hundred-man Indian ambulance corps.

In 1901, Gandhi returned to India, only to be quickly recalled to South Africa, where the plight of the Indian community had worsened in his brief absence. In 1903, Gandhi started the journal *Indian Opinion* and, a year later, founded the Phoenix commune in an effort to put into practice a utopian scheme he had read about in John Ruskin's 1860 essay "Unto This Last." The Phoenix community would be established on three principles: that the good of the individual is contained in the good of all, that all work is equally valuable, and that only a life of labor is worth living.

Into this period of utopian experiment, the so-called Zulu Rebellion of 1906 intruded. Once again, Gandhi acted out of a sense of loyalty to the British Empire and organized another ambulance corps, which ended up treating far more wounded Zulus than British soldiers. The project, begun because of his perceived allegiance to the British crown, instead opened his eyes to the cruelty of which the empire was capable. As he worked to aid the casualties of the war, Gandhi's thoughts turned to *brahmacharya*, the Hindu quest for self-realization. This, in turn, gave rise to his embrace of *satyagraha*, the hungering quest for truth.

Immersed in these twin themes, Gandhi organized a nonviolent campaign in 1907 to overturn the newly enacted Transvaal Asiatic Registration Act (TARA), a South African law requiring Indians living in the Transvaal to be fingerprinted and issued government registration certificates that had to be carried with them at all times. This was the first of what would be called "satyagraha campaigns," in which nonviolent civil disobedience was used to compel the government to remove onerous and oppressive measures. Under Gandhi's direction, virtually the entire South African Indian community refused to obey the registration law. When authorities ordered him to leave the colony, Gandhi refused and was jailed–as were thousands of Indians, who soon became a heavy burden on the South African prisons. At last, General Jan Smuts, South Africa's premier, made a compromise with Gandhi, repealing the registration law in exchange for voluntary submission to registration. Gandhi agreed, but a mob of Indian extremists who were angered by the compromise attacked Gandhi when he came forward to register himself. Beaten unconscious, he narrowly escaped death. His first question upon his recovery was about the leader of the mob that had attacked him. Learning that the leader was in custody, Gandhi appealed to authorities for his immediate release.

In 1908, after voluntary registration began, Smuts reneged on his agreement with Gandhi by refusing to repeal TARA and enforcing another law, the Transvaal Immigration Restriction Act (TIRA), which barred most Indians from even entering Transvaal. In response, Gandhi led public burnings of the voluntary registration certificates and encouraged illegal crossings of the Transvaal border. Thousands were jailed.

Settling in for a prolonged struggle, Gandhi secured 1,100 acres outside of Johannesburg and planted there the Tolstoy Farm as a communal center of resistance and self-sufficiency. At 6:30 on the morning of November 6, 1913, in protest of a tax imposed on Indians, Gandhi commenced the "Great March" of 2,200 men and women in a mass illegal border crossing, which focused worldwide attention on the situation in South Africa. Again, thousands were arrested–including Gandhi–and thousands more went on strike. Gandhi's activities in South Africa inspired a popular movement in India, which compelled the Indian government to lodge an official protest with the South African government. Under international pressure, Smuts yielded, repealed the tax, and relaxed the immigration laws.

Having emerged as a remarkable leader of change in South Africa, Gandhi returned to India in January 1915 and toured the country, determined to discover and reconnect with the vast country first-hand. In May 1915 he established the Satyagraha Ashram and, two years later, embarked on his first Indian satyagraha campaign to liberate the indigo tenant farmers of Champaran (a district in northern Bihar) from oppression under their planter landlords.

Gandhi aimed first at raising morale and instilling courage, rejecting conventional legal remedies because he believed that the farmers were so terrified of the landlords' power that they would be unable to press their case successfully. When the government responded to his speaking and organizing efforts by ordering him to leave the district, he refused, was arrested, and then summoned to court to answer charges. In a dramatic moment that received news coverage throughout the nation, Gandhi openly admitted his guilt and explained that his obedience was to the higher law of conscience. The case against him was ultimately dropped, and Gandhi and others traveled throughout the district recording statements from farmers. Their stories of hardship roused public opinion, moving the government to appoint a committee of inquiry in June 1917 to look into the landlord–tenant situation. In the end, the government compelled the landlord planters to make restitution to their tenant farmers. It was the first Indian triumph of the satyagraha principle.

In 1918, Gandhi led a new satyagraha in Ahmedabad. There, cotton mill laborers wanted a 50 percent increase in pay, whereas mill owners offered no more than 20 percent. Gandhi studied the issue and determined that 35 percent was reasonable, whereupon he organized a strike to obtain this raise. After two weeks without work, the striking workers began to waver, prompting Gandhi to undertake a fast as a means of applying moral pressure on the mill owners to accept arbitration. Unwilling to be responsible for the death of Gandhi, they agreed to binding arbitration and finally agreed to the 35 percent increase.

That year Gandhi also initiated the Kheda satyagraha, a campaign to persuade the government to suspend taxes levied on farmers struggling through a nationwide famine. Those who could not pay their taxes were threatened with foreclosure and loss of their land. Gandhi persuaded all farmers to withhold payment of taxes, and when seizure of crops was threatened, the farmers—again at Gandhi's urging—harvested their crops before the government could take them. Finally, in June, the government offered a compromise by which those farmers who could afford the tax would voluntarily pay it while those who could not were granted permission to suspend payment. Gandhi himself was not entirely pleased with the result, since he believed that no one should have to pay the tax in time of famine. Nevertheless, the campaign had a profound effect on the peasants, awakening them to the power of mass civil disobedience.

Following the Ahmedabad and Kheda satyagrahas, the British government passed the Rowlatt Acts, which criminalized the possession of any antigovernment document with the "intention" of circulating it and gave police officials broad powers of search, seizure, and arrest, effectively suspending habeas corpus and other basic legal restraints. Although some provisions were dropped before the legislation was enacted in March 1919, Gandhi led a satyagraha against the Rowlatt measures that blossomed into India's first nationwide satyagraha campaign, in which Indians successfully halted the business of the entire nation.

The general paralysis stunned British officials, who responded by arresting Gandhi, an act that triggered violent mob demonstrations that in turn resulted in police violence, which served only to exacerbate the violence among demonstrators. Despite having been marred by violence, the demonstrations against the Rowlatt Acts made history as the first nationwide civil disobedience and as the high-water mark of cooperation between Muslims and Hindus.

Tragically, the triumphant campaign was followed by the infamous Amritsar Massacre. On April 13, 1919, British general Reginald Dyer attacked a mass meeting of some ten thousand in Amritsar at the Jallianwala Bagh, a ground of perhaps seven acres enclosed by a wall through which there were just five exits. Dyer sent troops and two armored cars, each with machine guns, into the Jallianwala Bagh and opened fire. According to unofficial reports, more than a thousand Indians were killed in the space of ten minutes.

The carnage and sheer cruelty of Amritsar turned Gandhi frankly against the British Empire. At the next meeting of the Indian National Congress, the so-called Amritsar Congress, Gandhi called for a new round of nonviolent resistance and urged the Congress to pass a resolution supporting the revival of traditional Indian hand spinning and hand weaving as alternatives to importing any British cloth. The Congress complied and also elected Gandhi as its chairman.

In the wake of Amritsar, the British government broke its pledge to support the Ottoman sultan of Turkey against the republican revolution that was seeking to overthrow him. Whatever else the oppressive Ottoman sultan might have been, he was revered by Muslims worldwide as the caliph, the head of international Islam. To contribute to his overthrow was interpreted as an attack on Islam. Gandhi supported Indian Muslims in protesting the decision to stop propping up the sultan, and he believed that all Indian Hindus should join in supporting the nation's Muslims. Having identified a cause that could unite the two great religions of India, Gandhi proposed what he called "non-cooperation" with the British government—a massive program of nonviolent civil disobedience that amounted to a large-scale boycott of British laws, institutions, mercantile concerns, and import merchandise. Thus Gandhi assumed leadership of a movement that collectively turned its back on Britain. He reasoned that a government with no one to govern was powerless.

Noncooperation quickly developed into a call for *swaraj*, or home rule. The swaraj movement encompassed the renunciation of all titles and honors conferred by the British government; a total boycott of law-courts, educational institutions, councils, elections, imported merchandise (especially foreign cloth), and all functions of government. Additionally, all Indians were to refuse conscription into the army. To replace what was being boycotted, Gandhi promoted a program of Indian national education and Indian home industries, especially the spinning and weaving of homespun.

Noncooperation inspired and swept the nation, bringing the people of India together as never before and shaking the British Empire to its core. By 1921, Indians bestowed on Mohandas Gandhi the title of Mahatma—roughly, "Great Soul"—and he was widely worshipped as a saint, messiah, or incarnation of God. The government responded in the only way it knew how: mass arrests. Thirty thousand Indians would become political prisoners by the end of the year.

The mass arrests enflamed India, and as violence broke out, Gandhi came to the realization that he had lost control of the movement. When a mob that included congressmen torched a police station in the town of Chauri Chaura on February 5, 1922, incinerating twenty-two officers, Gandhi appealed to the Congress to formally suspend the campaign. He himself was arrested, tried, and sentenced to six years' imprisonment for sedition.

Gandhi was released in 1924 for an appendectomy, having spent just two years behind bars. Then he fasted for three weeks that October in an effort to restore peace and return the movement to nonviolence. He also made an effort to redirect the energy of the resistance away from the British and toward the removal of untouchability. In the meantime, however, India was swept by labor strikes and revolutionary agitation that was often marked by violence. In February 1928, Gandhi judged that the time had come for a new satyagraha campaign.

The place was Bardoli in Gujarat, where land taxes had been sharply increased, and Gandhi gave his blessing to a movement that suspended payment of all taxes until the government reduced them to fair and reasonable rates. In response to the tax boycott, the government dished up a mixture of bribery, imprisonment, fines, violence, and land and cattle seizure. The Indians, in turn, expanded their boycott to encompass every department and activity of the government. Indian officials resigned en masse. Effectively rendered impotent, the government grudgingly agreed to release political prisoners, return seized lands, and render compensation for other property lost.

The success of the Bardoli movement combined with escalating resentment against the government moved the Indian National Congress to refocus effort from a struggle for home rule to a campaign for total independence. Gandhi believed the moment was now ripe for the launch of a new dramatic and completely nonviolent campaign: the Salt satyagraha.

When the British viceroy rejected eleven demands Gandhi had articulated as the essence of self-government, he decided to directly attack the salt law, which taxed salt—a staple of rich and poor alike—and also outlawed the manufacture of one's own salt as well as the purchase of untaxed domestic salt. Starting from Ahmedabad on March 12, 1930, Gandhi led a 240-mile march to the sea, where he intended publicly to break the law by "making salt"—that is, gathering natural sea salt that had crystallized under the sun on the beach. His fellow marchers numbered seventy-eight handpicked followers, whose progress was eagerly followed by Indians all along the route to Dandi, on the coast of the Arabian Sea. The event, which was widely covered by the press, thrilled the nation and electrified the world, and when Gandhi reached the ocean and picked up a fistful of salty mud on April 6, Indians began making and selling illegal salt everywhere. Gandhi and others were quickly rounded up, but their arrest only raised the pitch of resistance and increased the intensity of the world's focus on India, finally pressuring the viceroy into repealing the salt tax and other repressive measures.

At the height of his international prestige, Gandhi sailed to London, where he participated in the Round Table Conference of 1931 as the representative of the Indian National Congress. It soon became apparent to Gandhi that the conference was being held in bad faith and was little more than an effort to slow the momentum of the independence movement. Nevertheless, Gandhi made a point of visiting with unemployed textile mill workers who had lost their jobs because of the Indian boycott of imported cloth. Far from being resentful, they expressed love, support, and admiration. No sooner did Gandhi return to India, however, than he was told of the arrest of key movement leaders. Gandhi responded by informing the viceroy, Lord Willingdon, that the Indian National Congress would act to resist "measures of legalized Government terrorism." The viceroy, in turn, ordered Gandhi's arrest—he was picked up before dawn on January 4—along with the arrest of most other "instigators," and declared the Indian National Congress illegal.

As Gandhi foresaw, the new round of repression served only to harden the people's resolve. When British Prime Minister Ramsay MacDonald segregated India's lowest castes—called the "depressed classes" by British authorities—giving them separate electorates, Gandhi objected that it was an attempt to divide and destroy Hindu society and, in turn, India itself. He announced from prison a "fast unto death" beginning on September 20, 1932. The fast prompted many Hindu leaders to fight for the removal of untouchability, and a number of temples were suddenly opened to the Harijans ("untouchables," now referred to as Dalits). The British government was discovering that Gandhi was even more influential inside prison walls than out.

As Gandhi's health declined, the Poona Pact was concluded between the untouchables and upper-caste Hindus, which doubled the number of representatives apportioned to the lowest castes and abandoned the idea of separate electorates. Satisfied, Gandhi broke his fast, and with this objective achieved, he next turned his attention to an intensive campaign to remove untouchability once and for all.

■

When World War II began in September 1939, Britain took India into the struggle without so much as consulting Indian leaders, thereby igniting a crisis in which many members of the Indian National Congress resigned in protest. The remaining members attempted to exploit the situation by offering to help Britain in exchange for immediate self-rule. Gandhi did not endorse this bargain, arguing that it would taint independence with both violence and coercion. In any event, the British government rejected the offer, whereupon the Indian National Congress asked Gandhi to resume congressional leadership.

Returned to the helm, Gandhi launched a civil disobedience campaign against the curtailment of freedom in wartime. Some twenty-five thousand were arrested. When Japan joined World War II in December 1941 and posed an immediate threat to India, the British became anxious to find ways to quell dissent. Sir Stafford Cripps was dispatched by the government to discuss establishing dominion status for India, which would have given the individual Indian states and provinces the authority to secede after the war and to draft a nonbinding constitution. However, Gandhi and the Congress rejected the proposal on several grounds, the most important of which was the potential it had for dismembering India.

With the failure of the Cripps mission, the Indian National Congress passed a "Quit India" resolution on August 8, 1942, definitively setting total independence as its sole acceptable objective. To this, the government responded by arresting Gandhi and others, an action that incited a popular uprising against the already beleaguered British administration. Having jailed Gandhi and his followers—the chief enforcers of nonviolence—the government soon had violent demonstrations to contend with. Nevertheless, the incipient rebellion was quelled.

In the meantime, Gandhi remained in jail, and on February 22, 1944, Kasturba—also in custody—succumbed to pneumonia. Brokenhearted, Gandhi suffered a decline in his health, which prompted British authorities, who feared the consequences of his dying in their custody, to release him in May of that year.

The end of World War II in September 1945 brought the Labour Party, whose members favored Indian decolonization, into power in Britain. With this, the momentum toward Indian independence increased rapidly. The new government dispatched a Cabinet Mission to work with Indian leaders on the creation of an interim government and to make a plan for the final transfer of power from Britain to an independent Indian authority. The Cabinet Mission proposed dividing India into three provincial groups, one dominated by a Hindu majority, the other two by Muslim majorities. In certain areas of power—such as defense and foreign affairs—a "Central Authority" would govern, but in other areas of power, each group would be free to write its own constitution. Gandhi vehemently objected to this dismemberment of India. India's Muslims, as represented by the Muslim League, were most concerned with claiming Pakistan as a nation independent from both Britain and India. This demand overrode the Cabinet Mission's proposal and provoked violent rioting throughout India—especially in Calcutta, where thousands were killed in the space of four bloody days. Shortly thereafter, a horrified Gandhi resumed his unification efforts, walking from house to house, barefoot, to talk and to listen to Hindus as well as Muslims.

The direct approach proved effective for a time, but India, on the verge of independence, also hung on the precipice of civil war. To avert this, Congress agreed—over Gandhi's pleas—to partition India by creating an independent Pakistan. While some celebrated independence on August 15, 1947, Gandhi campaigned to restore peace. As Calcutta erupted in new violence, he began his final "fast unto death," a physical and moral protest that shamed the city's Hindus and Muslims into making peace.

■

The price Gandhi paid for working on behalf of India rather than exclusively for Hindus or for Muslims was high. Despite his opposition to the partition, Hindu extremists believed he was a traitor who had sacrificed Hindu interests in his efforts to appease the Muslim minority. As violence between these religious groups continued to escalate, so did the attempts on his life. Despite a bomb incident at one of his regular prayer meetings, Gandhi refused to allow fear of death to get in the way of his mission to unite Muslims and Hindus.

At 5:10 in the afternoon of January 30, 1948, Gandhi walked out onto the lawn of Birla House, where he was living in New Delhi, to join about five hundred others in prayers. Weakened by fasts and his many struggles, he supported himself on the shoulders of his "walking sticks": grandniece-in-law Abha and grandniece Manu. As often happened, the adoring crowd pressed toward him to touch his garment or his feet. As Gandhi paused and folded his hands in the traditional Hindu *namaste* salutation, Nathuram Vinayak Godse, a Hindu extremist, stepped out from the crowd. He greeted Gandhi, then drew a pistol, which he fired three times at close range. The rounds hit Gandhi in the chest and abdomen, and he crumpled to the ground.

Many Hindus insist that Mahatma died with "Hey Ram" (Oh God) on his lips. Others recall only a sigh, or perhaps the single syllable "Ah"—an expression neither Hindu nor Muslim, intelligible to everyone, everywhere.

It was a death both tragic and poignant, but it was an end Gandhi himself always accepted as a likelihood. He would have counseled his followers that it hardly mattered, that only the work of his life counted. This was the course and creed of the "servant leader," willing both to magnify and dedicate his individual presence to advance the enterprise, even as he subordinated the demands of his ego to achieve that very goal. A leader to the end, Gandhi created a standard for all who would manage transformative change in any collective endeavor.

■

Deciding

Gandhi measured all decision against the truth. Slavery, oppression, injustice, violence—all were untruthful because they extorted belief and forced compliance; therefore, these evils were to be avoided or opposed. Yet it is one thing to decide what is truthful in one's own life and quite another, as a leader, to make decisions governing the collective life that is a company, corporation, or other enterprise. Gandhi, affectionately called *bapu* (Hindi for "father") by his followers, made the decisions for a vast movement and for an even vaster people. The stakes could not have been higher: The fate of many individual lives and the Indian nation itself hung in the balance.

The six lessons here include advice on harnessing your imagination as a litmus test—or talisman—for decision making; knowing how far you can press popular leadership; the importance and persuasive power of transparency in the decision-making process; when to compromise and when to draw a line; and how to build and maintain the courage to make decisions and to follow them through, against doubters and other opposition.

Lesson 1
PUT A FACE ON POLICY

"Whenever you are in doubt . . . apply the following test."

~ August 1947

To an unidentified correspondent who had expressed uncertainty about which action to take in a difficult situation, Gandhi offered what he called a "talisman." In actuality, it was a litmus test to be used in evaluating a decision or policy. When in doubt, he advised the correspondent, call to mind "the face of the poorest and the weakest man whom you may have seen, and ask yourself if the step you contemplate is going to be of any use to him."

For Gandhi, the litmus test of any proposed action was how it would affect the most vulnerable individual imaginable. The test was therefore human and particular, never ideological and general. His assumption was that if the contemplated step was likely to improve the lot of the lowest—again, imagined as a particular person—it would benefit everyone.

"Company policy" is too often used as a substitute for actual, individual decision making concerning actual individuals. The customer service rep who responds to a client's complaint by taking refuge in "company policy" rather than addressing the impact of a *particular* transaction on this *particular* person is practicing very bad business and is likely to cost the company numerous customers, albeit one at a time. Gandhi advised testing policy against individuals. If the policy passed the test, it was a good policy. If it failed, it was in need of change. He rejected the practice of forcing individuals to conform to policy.

Political ideologists such as Lenin, Mao Zedong, and Stalin were always willing to sacrifice people to policy. "A single death is a tragedy, a million deaths is a statistic," Stalin famously declared in defense of ideologically driven war. Gandhi was never willing to consider his policies in terms of statistics—they all bore a human expression. Follow Stalin or follow Gandhi: The choice is yours. Just bear in mind that the people who do business with you—external and internal customers alike—also have a choice.

■

Lesson 2
GET READY TO BE A LONELY LEADER

> "It is a superstition and ungodly thing to believe that an act of a
> majority binds a minority."
>
> ~ "Passive Resistance," *Hind Swaraj*, 1909

Some CEOs are autocrats, others are democrats. Neither extreme is an optimal leadership policy. To impose an authoritarian will on the members of an organization is to treat them as functionaries rather than as thinking human beings. Quite apart from the damage this does to individual morale, such a policy is a bad bargain for management because it fails to make full use of the company's costly human assets. Consider two workers: They are both paid the same salary; one uses 100 percent of her talent, the other 10 percent. Which worker represents the greater value for the company? The answer is self-evident, of course, yet authoritarian managers will fully sacrifice 90 percent of the value of their human capital when, by reflexively and inflexibly imposing their policies and procedures, they fail to allow an individual to use, to express, and to act on his or her uniquely valuable perspective and talent.

The democratic CEO, whose leadership is based on bending to the expressed will of the members of the organization, makes a different kind of mistake by her unquestioning assumption that the majority should prevail. Is her objective to please as many of her employees as possible? Or is it a belief that the majority is more likely to get a given issue right than the minority?

If the first answer is correct for a given CEO, we should question whether pleasing one's employees is even a valid goal for an enterprise. Is it likely to produce a profit, let alone the best possible profit? Almost certainly not. More valid goals might include creating customer satisfaction, producing a worthwhile product, and creating shareholder value. All of these—and preferably some combination of these—are more likely to contribute to productive sustainability than aiming to please the members of the organization.

Growing a productive and profitable enterprise is the surest way to create satisfaction among all the constituents of a company—especially the workers, whose ongoing livelihood depends on the ongoing success of the firm. Yet to achieve and sustain profitability, the CEO may from time to time have to make decisions that run contrary to the expressed will of the majority of his employees.

So be it. There is nothing sacrosanct or even inherently valuable about thoughtlessly bowing to the majority. It is also a fallacy to assume that the majority is more likely than the minority to be right. The classic refutation of this belief is the historical example of the many centuries during which the majority was convinced that the world was flat.

In the end, a leader must act with the well-being of every stake-holder in mind. This may mean sometimes making unpopular decisions, and it very often requires departing from the perceived wisdom of the majority by relying instead on advice from qualified experts or on your own understanding of the issues. Leadership, it is often said, can feel very lonely. The reason for this is simple: Leadership *is* lonely. Done right, it comes down to the decision of a single, solitary human being. Every other attitude, belief, or policy relating to leadership is either subordinate to this truth or is an instance of self-delusion.

■

Lesson 3
EMBRACE TRANSPARENCY

> "Nothing . . . should be done secretly. This is an open rebellion.
> In this struggle secrecy is a sin."
>
> ~Speech at AICC (All-India Congress Committee) meeting,
> August 8, 1942

Identity theft, online fraud, compromised passwords, and industrial espionage—all of these are very real security risks for many businesses. Every business, like every individual, must maintain a certain amount of confidentiality in everyday transactions. But as a management strategy, secrecy is counterproductive. It undermines trust and raises suspicion throughout the organization. Even worse, it discourages people from feeling that they have any significant stake in the enterprise. In contrast, transparency builds trust and invites a sense of ownership among everyone in the organization. Gandhi ensured that everything he did was an episode in what he called an "open rebellion." Each act of civil disobedience was public—a *demonstration* of disobedience. The very *transparency* of the revolution he led was the *secret* of its success.

But can *you* dispense with secrecy?

Probably not entirely. In some areas, confidentiality is absolutely required to thwart everything from embezzlement to espionage. In other areas, it may well be positively desirable. For example, as a means of forestalling unnecessary jealousies and internecine strife, most companies either discourage or explicitly forbid employees to discuss their salaries with one another. But in many operational areas, there is no real need for secrecy.

The right move is to review your policies with an eye toward introducing full transparency wherever possible. Policies based on or promoting secrecy are typically products of reflex and habit. We find it easier simply to withhold information than to devote time and intelligence to deciding what to make public and what to keep close. For this reason, examine the motivation behind your non-transparent policies and practices. If you yourself find the motives unpersuasive, shed the policies. You'll do better without them.

■

Lesson 4
DEFINE YOUR NO-COMPROMISE ZONES

> "I am an uncompromising opponent of violent methods even to serve the noblest of causes. There is, therefore, really no meeting ground between the school of violence and myself."
>
> ~ "My Path," *Young India*, December 11, 1924

The Russian revolutions of 1917 overthrew Czar Nicholas II and ushered in a communist ("Bolshevik") government. By 1924, Gandhi had become wary of Bolshevik attempts to obtain his endorsement of their cause: "Those Bolshevik friends who are bestowing their attention on me should realize that however much I may sympathize with and admire worthy motives, I am an uncompromising opponent of violent methods even to serve the noblest of causes."

Leadership often requires compromise, and the would-be leader who arbitrarily forecloses all possibility of compromise is in all likelihood doomed to a brief, unhappy career. Nevertheless, every CEO and manager must stake out the areas on which there can be no compromise. These *no-compromise zones* should never be designated arbitrarily or from motives of ego, but should instead protect matters of principle and policy that have been proven to be vital to the operation or core identity of the enterprise.

For Gandhi, laudable ends could never justify violent means because such means contaminated even the noblest of objectives. While this meant that he would not lend his support to the Bolshevik revolution and its aftermath, both of which were stained by the blood of violence, it did not mean that he would cut off all contact with the Bolsheviks. As he explained, his "creed of non-violence," while it barred compromise, "not only does not preclude me but compels me even to associate with anarchists and all those who believe in violence. But the association is always with the sole object of weaning them from what appears to me to be their error." Never compromise on your no-compromise zone, but never confuse a refusal to compromise with a refusal to communicate.

■

Lesson 5
CULTIVATE THE COURAGE OF CONVICTION

> "For the last twenty years we have tried to learn not to lose courage even when we are in a hopeless minority and are laughed at. We have learned to hold on to our beliefs in the confidence that we are in the right."
> ~Speech at AICC (All-India Congress Committee) meeting,
> August 8, 1942

Your task is not simple. You want to make decisions based on the best possible information, expert advice, and your own intelligence, perception, and intuition. You also want to be open to other points of view, including the consensus of your organization. You want to be neither an unthinking autocrat nor an unthinking democrat. You don't want to lead in the blind conviction that you and only you are right, but neither do you want to lead by following the majority.

Like all leaders of complex enterprises, Gandhi faced this very problem of balance in decision making. For most of his career, the majority scorned the idea of Indian self-rule, let alone independence, and scoffed at the method of passive resistance. It is supremely difficult to face down this kind of challenge, to maintain your belief that you are right when almost everyone else says that you are wrong. Seeing yourself as constituting a "hopeless minority" can quickly lead to, well, hopelessness. The only defense against this emotion, as Gandhi saw it, was "to cultivate . . . courage of conviction," one of the keenest tools in a leader's toolbox. Like any edged implement, however, it cuts both ways and can be used for good or ill. Maintaining against the opinion of the majority an erroneous, even destructive belief requires the same courage of conviction as maintaining a valid and valuable position against that majority tide. Courage of conviction is as indispensable to a leader as a razor-sharp chisel to an artist working wood or stone, but not even the most exquisitely honed tool is sufficient unto itself. It must be employed with skill and careful judgment and on the basis of as much knowledge as it is possible to obtain. As a sculptor must understand in detail the subject he models, so a leader must have a clear and accurate conception of his objectives and goals.

Doubt is an enemy of courage, but it is an aid to decision making. The most successful decision makers balance doubt and courage by breaking down the decision-making process into three broad phases.

In Phase 1, the leader collects data, including as many points of view on the issue as possible. He listens to the majority as well as the minority. He invites disagreement and dissent—which he welcomes and never penalizes. He calls for argument, even protest. Doubt is a principal driver of this phase.

Phase 2 is the evaluation process. The leader considers all of the data and opinions he has gathered. He may go back to some of his sources during this phase to ask for elaboration or feedback. By the end of this phase, he has formulated his decision.

In Phase 3, the decision is announced, explained as may be required, and put into execution. During this phase, the leader casts aside the doubt that served him well in Phase 1 and robustly embraces the courage of his convictions. Now is not a time to solicit minority or majority opinions. Once the decision has entered Phase

3, there is no longer room for doubt or dissent. The leader leads for wholly unified action and relies on wholehearted, cheerful compliance and collaboration from the entire organization.

■

Lesson 6
MAKE TIME YOUR ALLY

"I do not expect my views to be accepted all of a sudden."
~ "How Can India Become Free?" *Hind Swaraj*, 1909

Business communication moves at a digital tempo. There was a time when phone calls demanded an instant answer, but now they are routinely routed to voicemail. Emails and instant messages, however, are not so easily put off. We are relentlessly bombarded with demands for decisions and information. Time, always in short supply, is now taken for granted as an enemy. Not only are we expected to furnish virtually instantaneous answers to often complex questions, we ourselves expect to persuade others instantaneously as well.

The sense of urgency pervading business today is driven in large part by technology. When the most advanced form of long-distance communication was the letter, technology bought managers and CEOs valuable time. Letters required time to compose and time to be delivered. The benefit of this technological limitation was time to think. Digital technology has sped communication but also eliminated the benefit of added time.

When the stakes of a decision are high, it is prudent to avoid being goaded by technology into instantaneous communication. It goes without saying that allies are better than enemies, so why not enlist time as an ally rather than regard it as an enemy? As a shaper of public opinion and creator of social change, Gandhi defined the *expression* of his views as his "duty." As for *persuasion*, he was confident that "time can be trusted to do the rest" by allowing his expressed views to be digested, discussed, disseminated, evaluated, and acted upon. Gandhi enlisted time itself as an ally in his campaign for Indian independence.

Today, the technology of communication moves faster than the speed of thought. We must not forget that the proper function of technology is to serve thought, not to master it. CEOs and managers today face problems similar to those encountered by the first generations of workers who confronted the emerging technology of mass production and the automated assembly line. Those who study the nature of labor in early factories typically write about "men serving machines." The phrase is not intended as a moral or philosophical observation but as a literal description. Increasingly, through the late nineteenth century and into the twentieth, human beings "tended" or "served" machines, feeding raw material into them and pulling finished products out. The machines set the pace. The machines determined what human actions were required. The so-called post-industrial age that began in the late twentieth century saw a struggle to rebalance the relationship between technology and humanity. The ideal was to return technology unambiguously to the service of people. In today's offices, however, we are increasingly allowing technology, once again, to set the pace.

Harried CEOs serve their email inboxes, whether on desktop computers, laptops, or data-capable cell phones. Accessibility is valuable, but it comes at a high cost in expectations both perceived and actual. With the four brick-and-mortar walls of the traditional office crumbling, we are never quite sure how available we are expected to be—so more and more of us assume that we are expected to be available as close to 24/7 as possible. We think of this availability as the equivalent of rendering excellent service and creating a twenty-first-century level of customer satisfaction. But consider: A reflexively instantaneous response to every question, every problem, every issue shorts both you and your customer—

whether she is a client, a colleague, or some other stakeholder in your enterprise—on the most valuable commodity of all: time. An effective solution—an answer whose persuasive power requires thought to formulate—is far more valuable than a poor solution, no matter how rapidly it has been delivered.

Gandhi believed the problems of India were urgent. One day without home rule, he understood, was one more day of injustice inflicted and suffered. Yet he also believed time was a necessary ingredient to successful persuasion—persuasion with meaningful and enduring results. Many of us are driven by our sense of a shortage of time. Being thus driven, we do not feel free to unleash our full creativity and, thus deprived, are resentful—resentful toward those who make demands on us and resentful toward time itself. To say the least, such feelings are counterproductive.

The best CEOs possess the confidence to trust rather than to resent time. They enlist it as an ally in leadership by using technology as a tool rather than allowing themselves to become a tool of technology. Restoring this balance between mind and machine requires a surprisingly strenuous exercise of character and self-confidence, but the workout, vigorous though it may be, is well worth the effort.

Do or Die

Gandhi's quest for nonviolent change was never without violence or the threat of violence against him and his followers. He repeatedly exhorted those who joined the movement to look forward to death in the campaign just as a soldier marches to battle prepared to die. This man of peace motivated his followers the way generals and conquerors have motivated their armies and hordes: with the stark choice to do or die—in Hindi, *karo ya maro*.

The seven lessons in this chapter are devoted to the art of motivating without middle ground. They present principles for prompting maximum effort in situations that offer the highest stakes, the greatest risks, and the greatest opportunities. These are the leadership scenarios that lie beyond the complacency of the everyday and the ordinary. These are occasions of stark choices, in which failure is a distinct possibility but not an option and in which opportunity can be truly transformative.

Lesson 7
DON'T WAIT

> "I will not wait till I have converted the whole society to my view
> but will straightaway make a beginning with myself."
> ~Constructive Workers' Conference, January 24, 1946

If there is one universal set of facts that the life and work of Mohandas Gandhi proves beyond any possibility of doubt, it is that a single person can bring change, that change—even the greatest change—begins with a single person, and that the change begins the moment that person begins it. Nowhere in this sequence of facts is *waiting* an option. If you mean to make a difference in the world or in your company, you cannot wait for others to begin the change, and you cannot wait even for your own changes to become widespread, let alone universal. Begin the project, no matter how ambitious, with yourself. Begin now.

■

Lesson 8
NO STRATEGY WITHOUT TACTICS

> "That will leave us just where we are."
> ~ "Pure Swadeshi," Navajivan, July 11, 1920

Gandhi advocated *swadeshi,* the Hindi term for self-sufficiency, as an alternative to India's economic dependence on goods imported from Britain. Political independence, he argued, could not be achieved in the absence of economic independence. Thus swadeshi was an important strategy for achieving Indian nationhood.

Strategic thinking is crucial for any CEO, but you must not stop thinking just because you have finally formulated a strategy. Military commanders have long understood that even the most brilliant strategy is useless—even destructive—without good tactics to execute it effectively. Any general's planning must dig below the level of strategy to tactics. In the case of swadeshi, Gandhi proposed (among other things) ending Indian dependence on imported cotton by weaving cotton in India. It was a good idea—a good strategy—but Gandhi penetrated beneath the concept to its execution and found that Indian cotton mills could not produce enough cloth to meet Indian needs for "the immediate future." He then dug into this fact and learned that their "weaving capacity is greater than their spinning capacity." One solution proposed to correct this imbalance was to use imported yarn rather than imported cloth. While it was true that imported yarn was cheaper than imported cloth, the result would still be "large imports, not of cloth, but of yarn. That will leave us just where we are. We need not believe that we shall be saving on weaving, for yarn will cost more. This," Gandhi concluded, "is not swadeshi."

What was needed were more effective tactics for executing the strategy of swadeshi. Gandhi proposed the reestablishment of traditional hand spinning and hand weaving throughout India's homes. In this way, each household would produce only the yarn it could weave into cloth, and this cloth would fill the gap between what the commercial Indian mills could produce self-sufficiently and what India needed. No importation would be necessary.

Indeed, Gandhi wanted to promote traditional handicrafts beyond fulfilling mere subsistence needs. "It is," he wrote in 1920, "my suggestion to all lovers of swadeshi and to all owners of swadeshi stores that they should get women to spin and should popularize the cloth woven out of the yarn they produce." Typically, strategy is easy relative to tactics. "I know that this work [of hand spinning] is difficult and heart-breaking. But no progress is ever possible without venturing on a path beset with difficulties. The way to the Dhaulagiri peak is strewn with the bones of countless travelers."

Western business models typically stratify companies into upper management, which is charged with creating the "big picture" strategy, and middle management, whose job it is to formulate the tactics by which upper management's strategy is to be executed. Too often, this corporate structure divorces strategy from tactics, resulting in an imperfect fit—if not a total misfit—between idea and execution. Strategy must never be formulated without simultaneously creating tactics. At the very least, this requires close collaboration between upper and middle management, between the strategists and the tacticians. It is far better for the CEO to integrate strategy and tactics into the planning from the beginning. This approach has the brightest prospects for creating the best fit between concept and execution. If, in the process, it courts charges of micromanagement, so be it. Take the heat.

■

Lesson 9
HARNESS THE ENERGY OF IMPERFECTION

> "Man will ever remain imperfect, and it will always be his part to
> try to be perfect."
>   ~Interview with Nirmal Kumar Bose, November 9–10, 1934

You may live your entire life without ever encountering a kinesiologist—a student of the scientific study of human movement—but if you do, ask him to define "walking." You will discover that, from the kinesiologist's point of view, even the most graceful stride is neither more nor less than a process of falling and recovering from the fall. Walking may therefore be defined as continually falling forward. In a human being, perfect balance means standing still, whereas locomotion requires repeated cycles of relinquishing and regaining one's balance. The very means by which we make progress is a product of our imperfection.

Gandhi's entire life work is a demonstration that forward progress requires both preparedness for failure and strength for recovery. Do not hesitate to set perfection as the goal of your organization, but, in so doing, you must also recognize that only imperfection will move you and your enterprise toward that goal. For this reason, never criticize imperfection. Nurture it. Exploit it. Manage it. It is the fuel that drives every worthwhile endeavor.

Lesson 10
STAY DISSATISFIED

> "The goal ever recedes from us. . . . Satisfaction lies in the effort, not in the attainment. Full effort is full victory."
> ~ "Non-violence," *Young India*, March 9, 1922

The best CEOs conduct only unfinished symphonies. Goals exist to inspire ambitious aspiration, not to be attained, and if you ever find your organization nearing its goal, figure out a way to move the goal post. Satisfaction is a dangerous thing for dynamic enterprises. It is far better to stay dissatisfied—or to recognize, as Gandhi advised, that true satisfaction lies in the effort rather than in the attainment. Reward the members of your enterprise for their hard work, even as you build greater challenges for them. For your motto, reject "SUCCESS"; instead, adopt "STRIVE."

Lesson 11
THE TRAGEDY OF TIME LOST

> "After we had stolen fifteen minutes from people's time, we realized our foolishness and thanked God for opening our eyes."
> ~ Letter to Narandas Gandhi, July 28–31, 1930

In a letter to his kinsman and colleague Narandas Gandhi, Mohandas Gandhi related an anecdote about having wasted fifteen minutes in "a discussion on how to economize in the use of cloth-lined envelopes and save the same envelopes for use again and again. The question was whether to paste a blank sheet on the whole side of the envelope or paste only slips over portions where something was written. This was a futile discussion."

On reflection, Gandhi was appalled by this squandering of a quarter-hour "of beautiful time," a waste he characterized as a violation of truth and *ahimsa* (nonviolence), as well as a shameful display of a "lack of discrimination." Truth was violated, he said, "because the discussion was not inspired by an ardent desire for its [truth's] search," and "ahimsa was shamed" because time that should have been devoted to discovering the "sufferings of the people and in thinking about ways of ending them" was misspent on a futile discussion over a trivial matter.

The loss of fifteen minutes seemed to Gandhi a tragedy.

Considering that time is the one absolute commodity, his interpretation may not be as melodramatic and over the top as it first appears. While business professionals are accustomed to accounting for and auditing the expenditure of money, even more care should be devoted to tracking time. Time is entirely nonrenewable, and whether spent, invested, or simply lost, it is consumed. There is at least a chance of recovering money that has been misspent or lost, but time lost is lost forever, and irrecoverable loss is the very essence of tragedy. If, as a manager or CEO, you take seriously your responsibility for allocating your organization's time, consider cultivating Gandhi's sense of tragedy when it comes to the danger of squandering your most precious and limited resource.

■

Lesson 12
EXPECT SUCCESS

"I must not contemplate darkness before it stares me in the face."

~ "Independence," *Harijan,* July 28, 1946

On the verge of India's independence, Gandhi was asked to present his alternative should the main governing body—the so-called Constituent Assembly—fail. His response was a refusal to "contemplate darkness" before it actually stared him in the face. It was the poetic equivalent of the familiar "we'll cross that bridge when we come to it."

It is never a good leadership strategy to ignore potential problems, to fail to evaluate risks, to willfully refuse to anticipate pitfalls, or to turn your back on contingency planning. However, it is an invariably fatal strategy to allow the anticipation of trouble to paralyze you or your enterprise. Hope is not a substitute for strategy, but rather a necessary ingredient in any worthwhile strategic plan. The goal is to create a strategy that makes possible and facilitates the very best that you dare to hope for. At the same time, you must plan for contingencies—without allowing your contingency plans to trump or trample the hope. The anticipation of crisis will create crisis, if you allow it to blind you to the opportunity. The best attitude is to embark with the expectation of success, not failure.

■

Lesson 13

BE MISERLY WITH YOUR INSPIRATIONAL CURRENCY

"Here is a mantra, a short one, that I give you. You may imprint it on your hearts and let every breath of yours give expression to it. The mantra is: 'Do or Die.'"

~Speech at AICC (All-India Congress Committee) meeting, August 8, 1942

Do or die. Can there be any call to greater dedication than this? It marked the final phase of Gandhi's leadership of the "non-cooperation" movement. Years of struggle had persuaded him that a worthwhile cause required absolute dedication, without any halfway measures. And yet, should you, as a manager, emulate Gandhi's either/or absolutism? Can it even be emulated in a business context?

The answer to both questions is a qualified "no" and a qualified "yes." In most situations, the choice between doing and dying is false—at best, a spectacular exaggeration of a dilemma that is only apparent. Approach each task by asking for this degree of dedication, and you will soon find your treasury of inspirational capital inflated like certain Third World currencies: to the point of worthlessness.

Yet there are those rare, truly critical junctures in business life where "do or die" comes very close to expressing the stakes of the choices at hand and the degree of dedication required to choose and successfully navigate to the right choices. There are junctures in which the very survival of the business is at stake and in which nothing less than maximum effort is likely to prevail. Therefore, save your calls to absolute commitment and total dedication for these occasions. Be miserly when you spend your inspirational currency in its highest denominations. You never know when you will really need it—every bit of it.

The Genius of
Noncooperation

Noncooperation was both a general tactic Gandhi introduced for undermining the oppressive authority of the British Raj (government) in India and a specific phase in the movements for Indian home rule and independence. The idea behind both aspects of noncooperation was organized, nonviolent mass civil disobedience, the thrust of which would be less the breaking of British law (although this was necessary) than the ignoring of British law and British institutions in India ranging from law courts to various mercantile concerns. Gandhi understood that the authority of even the most oppressive government ultimately came from the consent of the governed. If the people turned their backs on the government, it would be powerless.

The government's adoption of the Defence of India Act in 1915 was aimed at curtailing "revolutionary activities" during World War I. By silencing protest, the act also encouraged the most tradition-bound members of Indian society to maintain long-accepted social structures and practices that retarded social progress. Chief among these was the enforcement of a strict caste system, including the "untouchability" of the lowest caste.

No sooner did the war end than, in 1919, passage of the Rowlatt Acts threatened to transform British India into an outright police state, as habeas corpus was suspended indefinitely and police were given virtual carte blanche to make searches, seizures, and arrests without warrant and, indeed, without necessarily showing cause. Moreover, British taxation and trade policies were keeping Indian farmers in acute poverty, which in turn created a host of physical and social ills, from endemic disease to illiteracy.

In the midst of these oppressive measures, Gandhi led a concentrated campaign of noncooperation in the rural Ahmedabad and Kheda districts, where farmers were languishing in acute poverty while government regulations compelled them to grow cash crops—for which they received almost nothing—instead of the subsistence food crops they desperately needed. The crisis of oppression was compounded by a famine, despite which the government refused to relent in its demand for full payment of regularly levied taxes. Gandhi banded together the farmers in a universal refusal to cooperate with the government. The required crops were not grown, and taxes went unpaid. The protest was so widespread that the colonial government was compelled to agree to suspend taxes during the famine, to permit farmers to grow the crops they wanted and needed, to restore lands seized from local farmers, and to release all those arrested during the noncooperation protest. It was an extraordinary victory over the British Empire—and, until April 13, 1919, largely unmarred by violence. On that day, a meeting among Indian Muslims convened at Jallianwala Bagh in Amritsar to protest the government's support of Mustafa Kemal (Atatürk), who had overthrown the Ottoman sultan—whom Muslims revered as the caliph (head) of Islam—was set upon by Anglo-Indian troops under General Reginald Dyer. In a slaughter involving machine guns and armored cars, hundreds of Indians (unofficial sources claimed more than a thousand) perished and many more were gravely wounded. Amritsar moved Gandhi to organize a nationwide noncooperation movement aimed at overturning the Rowlatt Acts once and for all. Offices, factories, and stores were shuttered. Gandhi exhorted Indians to withdraw from every British institution and to boycott all British imports.

National noncooperation shook the British Empire to its core as it inspired millions of Indians, but clashes between protesters and British authorities continued. After the Chauri Chaura incident in February of 1922, in which a mob set fire to a police station and incinerated twenty-two officers inside, Gandhi appealed for an end to the violence—which also meant suspending noncooperation. To secure the compliance of his followers and the Indian people, he staged a fast, in effect threatening to end his own life if the resistance did not come to a peaceful conclusion. Gandhi starved himself for three weeks. Although the main phase of noncooperation came to an end, both the principle and the tactic remained an active weapon in the arsenal of nonviolent civil disobedience.

For the business leader of today, noncooperation is a stark reminder of the need to do far more than order their employees about. A complex business enterprise cannot be run on forced obedience. Voluntary cooperation—self-direction toward common goals—is required, and it is the task of CEOs and managers to secure it day by day.

■

Lesson 14
COOPERATION MUST BE EARNED

> "If the people non-cooperate, what can a raja, a zamindar or a capitalist do?"
>
> ~ "Question Box," *Harijan*, June 1, 1947

The zenith of Gandhi's campaign of passive resistance against the British Raj in India was "noncooperation," in which the people simply declined to have anything to do with British law and institutions in India. As a CEO or manager, you may believe that nonco-operation has no application to your business. After all, if an employee chooses not to cooperate—won't do his job—you can simply fire him. It would seem, then, that business presents so obvious and easy an antidote to noncooperation that this tactic could never become a serious weapon in a dispute between labor and management or staff and supervisors.

Such complacency is an illusion, perhaps a delusion.

To be sure, an employee who refuses to do the work assigned to him can be fired—and in most situations should be. But noncooper-ation in an employment context is more usually a matter of degree than a simple refusal to work. A discontented employee will find selective modes of noncooperation, which may or may not prompt or even merit dismissal, but will certainly reduce the effectiveness of the employee and the value he delivers to the company. Even worse, if discontent is pervasive throughout the organization, a low level of noncooperation may come to characterize the entire workforce, with results ranging from bad to disastrous. Even if you could, would you fire everybody? In such a case, what can even a raja do?

Company rules, company policy, the employee handbook, and common sense all firmly define your authority as well as the respon-sibility of each employee to respect it. But the fact is that your authority alone is insufficient to create cooperation throughout the organization. Full, effective, cheerful cooperation is *given*—not simply grabbed or delivered on demand. Certainly, it cannot be taken for granted.

Approach the leadership task in the knowledge that your authority goes only so far. Leadership that rests solely on authority can never create the degree of cooperation required to produce sus-tained excellence. This level of organizational performance requires a foundation of cooperation, which you must earn by respecting your staff, engaging them, challenging them, rewarding them, and listening to them. Without the perception of having a significant stake in the enterprise, there is no reason for members of the organization to offer their cooperation to the leadership.

■

Lesson 15
THE SHELL OF OBEDIENCE

> "If anybody asks me to bow down my head—I am an old man and anybody can push me or knock me down—but if I say, 'I won't,' the utmost he can do is to kill me."
>
> ~Speech at a Prayer Meeting, December 22, 1945

For Gandhi, the cardinal virtue was fearlessness. "If you could learn that," he declared, "nobody would be able to keep you down." People can be forced to do anything, but they cannot be forced to obey willingly. Indeed, *forced willingness* is a contradiction in terms—a logically impossible state.

Gandhi intended this great lesson, that voluntary obedience cannot be coerced, as a lesson for people seeking freedom. Yet it is also a significant lesson for leaders. The autocrat or tyrant who forces obedience gains nothing but forced compliance. This is a shoddy, dangerous, and overpriced commodity. It is shoddy because it is nothing more than a shell. Forced compliance is a show of obedience, outward and superficial, so thin that it will crack under the slightest pressure. For this reason, it is also dangerous. An organization built on coercion is designed to collapse. And yet, insubstantial as such an enterprise is, the shoddy, dangerous construction comes at a great price. Coercion must be continually maintained, lest it fall apart immediately. This requires a ceaseless application of main-strength force, the cost of which, in spent energy, is exorbitant.

Like everyone else, CEOs need to learn that forced obedience is folly—less than worthless. Only an organization built on voluntary compliance, in which the leaders earn the privilege of leadership every day from the consent of those they lead, is built to endure and to prosper. This is not just an "ideal" condition of leadership; it is a necessary one.

■

Lesson 16
BOYCOTT A BAD BARGAIN

> "A king cannot govern at all if he is not able to carry any section of his subjects with him. It follows from this that the fewer the subjects who co-operate with him, the less will be his authority."
> ~ "Non-Cooperation," *Navajivan,* July 4, 1920

Offered a bad bargain, the best thing to do is walk away from it. Don't argue. Don't cajole. Don't threaten. Just leave.

This was the thrust of Gandhi's campaign of noncooperation with British authority in India. To the degree possible, he urged the Indian people to boycott British goods, to boycott the law courts, and to have nothing to do with any other British colonial institution, including the legislatures on which Indian representatives normally served. To the obvious question, "What if unworthy people get elected because we do not come forward?" Gandhi answered, "If such people enter the legislatures, the Government will not be able to run the government of an awakened people and it will be laughed at." The point of the legislative boycott was not merely to keep Indian legislators out of British government, but to show "that it will be impossible for anybody to get elected in legislatures as [the people's] representatives." By boycotting British government and institutions, Gandhi did not intend to destroy them but to do worse: to leave them on exhibit as empty shells.

If you would retain your freedom to lead effectively, refuse to be placed on the horns of a dilemma. Offered a bad choice, choose nothing. Turn away from the choice and start walking. If you are pursued with a better offer, consider it. If not, find another deal partner. The most powerful bargaining chip you have is your mere presence at the table. Withdraw it, and you have made a powerful statement—and certainly one that is far preferable to beginning a negotiation already having conceded terms to the other party.

■

Lesson 17
OPT OUT OF ARGUMENT

> "It takes two to make a quarrel."
> ~ "The Condition of India (continued): The Hindus & the
> Mohomedans," *Hind Swaraj*, 1909

The best way to win an argument is to avoid it. This is not always possible or even desirable; there are, after all, some things that must or should be disputed. Any argument, however—even one that you win—consumes time and energy. Therefore, engage only in those few that are worth having.

"If I do not want to quarrel with a Mahomedan," wrote the Hindu Gandhi, "the latter will be powerless to foist a quarrel on me." Refusing to argue takes from your opponent the power of argument. Practice the art of depriving your opponent of a target. If he wants an argument, why give it to him? Why empower him? As Gandhi put it, "An arm striking the air will become disjointed."

CEOs often make the mistake of believing that their leadership is based on power. This belief forces them to apply power—or attempt to—at virtually every turn, the more publicly the better. They see argument as a means of imposing their will on others and an opportunity to wield power more visibly. The truth is that the leadership of any CEO is not based on power—an abstract commodity—but on results. More often than not, quarrels work against achieving genuinely powerful results. What profit is there in "winning" an argument, asserting your power over someone else, if you fail to produce the desired result in the process? Better to keep your eye on the ends, lest you allow means to interfere with and obscure them. Focus on results, and there will be less and less time for dispute. Leave argument to your rivals. Invest your time in creating excellence.

■

Lesson 18
USE SOCIAL JIU-JITSU

> ". . . three thousand Indians in South Africa after due notice to the Government of the Transvaal crossed the Transvaal border in 1914 in defiance of the Transvaal immigration law and compelled the Government to arrest them. When it failed to provoke them to violence or to coerce them into submission, it yielded to their demand."
>
> ~ "The Momentous Issue," *Young India*, November 10, 1921

The martial art known as "jiu-jitsu" is a collection of techniques by which you use an attacker's own energy against him. In effect, you put the opponent in a position to be defeated by his own strength. This is analogous to Gandhi's prescription for nonviolent civil disobedience. Oppressive states are prepared to deal with either violent resistance or total compliance, but they are powerless when they are confronted with nonviolent resistance or noncooperation. In the case of the 1914 protest in South Africa, the three thousand violators of the immigration law "compelled" the government to arrest them. Unlike the protestors, the government had no choice but to obey its own laws. Unlike the protestors, it was powerless to disobey. Moreover, when the resisters declined to offer violence—yet nevertheless refused to obey the law—the government authorities were at a loss as to how to treat them. In the end, it became more expedient for the government, a victim of its own power, to yield.

The application of social jiu-jitsu is often the most effective means of resolving disputes without escalating them into contests of wills. Consider the following management scenario. Joe supervises five employees, but, an inveterate micromanager, he insists on doing much of his department's work himself. This results in slow turnaround of projects, along with other inefficiencies. You have tried on several occasions to get Joe to mend his ways by asking him to put greater trust in his staff by giving them more responsibility, but your efforts have been to no avail. Rather than continuing to engage in a protracted struggle, you exercise social jiu-jitsu by giving Joe a raise along with significantly augmented responsibilities. Pleased with the promotion and the money, he digs into his new assignments in his habitual lone-wolf style—and, predictably, is soon overwhelmed. You allow the pressure to build and the work to pile up. You make no suggestions. Finally, on his own, Joe begins giving more of the work to his staff.

So the company has won. Joe has won. And, of course, *you* have won—but you continue to say absolutely nothing about it, except to tell Joe that his department is doing a great job, "even if things were a little rocky at the start."

■

Lesson 19
ENDS CANNOT JUSTIFY MEANS

> "Civil disobedience is never followed by anarchy. Criminal disobedience can lead to it."
>
> ~ "The Immediate Issue," *Young India*, January 5, 1922

Virtually lifelong, Gandhi's chief method of creating social and political change was to break the law, and yet he expressed his wish that he could persuade everybody that "civil disobedience is the inherent right of a citizen." He explained that whereas breaking the law through civil disobedience is never followed by anarchy, breaking the law through criminal disobedience "can lead to it." The difference between civil disobedience and criminal disobedience is that the practitioner of the former "never uses arms and hence . . . is harmless to a State that is at all willing to listen to the voice of public opinion." A civil resister is, however, "dangerous to an autocratic State, for he brings about its fall by engaging public opinion upon the matter for which he resists the State." In contrast to the civil resister, a criminal is actually or potentially violent—even if the violence is nothing more than, say, a swindle or other act of fraud—and therefore poses a real threat to any state, whether democratic, autocratic, or something in between.

Gandhi took great care to explain that merely breaking the law did not in itself constitute civil disobedience. The civil resister had to choose only the laws that needed to be broken, and he had to break them in ways that were wholly nonviolent, that preserved his morally harmless innocence. Introduce any violence or deception into the violation of the law, and civil resistance becomes nothing more or less than common criminality.

An effective leader leads for change but takes great pains to ensure that only the proper instruments of change are employed. Means and ends are inseparable. Violence, which in a business context encompasses deception, fraud, intimidation, and the like, cannot bring about a healthy, ethical, enduring change for the better because the enterprise will always be in bondage to the violence of its means. Whatever else it may be, change that results from violence is never liberation.

But what if the desired change can be achieved only through violence—through cheating, unethical, or even illegal means? *Ipso facto*, such change cannot give the organization the freedom to achieve greater things, and therefore efforts toward it should be abandoned before they are commenced.

Worst of all is the fact that even ostensibly good ends can be contaminated by the wrong choice of instrument—the choice of a dubious means—and such contamination will destroy any benefit the desired end might otherwise have offered.

Give Everyone a Stake

The Hindu culture of Gandhi's India was rigidly divided into four castes, from the scholarly Brahmins at the top to the laboring Shudras at the bottom. Below these castes was an "outcaste," the aforementioned Dalits. In Gandhi's time, about 20 percent of Indian Hindus were Dalits consigned to such menial and "unclean" labor as sweeping, latrine cleaning, leather tanning, and traditional hand spinning. These "untouchables" were deemed unfit for society and could not take water from public wells or even enter the Hindu temples. Indeed, at the time that social and political agitation against untouchability began in the 1920s, Dalits were not only barred from the temples but also from the roads leading to them. Those Dalits who strove to improve their lot through education and material advancement discovered that these efforts made no dent in the barriers posed against them. Virtually all were among the most impoverished of India's people.

Gandhi made the removal of untouchability a central focus of his campaign for human rights in India. By the early 1930s, the cause ran parallel with the ongoing movement toward Indian independence and was part of Gandhi's assault on the caste system—at least insofar as it enforced a rigid and confining social structure that, Gandhi believed, prevented India's full progress toward independence.

Orthodox Hindus cite the ancient Sanskrit Vedas—the oldest Hindu scriptures, dating from approximately 4000 BCE to 500 CE—as the source of and mandate for caste, but as Gandhi pointed out, the Rig-Veda, not only the oldest of the Hindu scriptures but the earliest known book, makes no mention of untouchability and very little reference to caste. Gandhi and many other scholars argued that caste was actually a development of the later Vedic period and evolved since then, not as a religious institution, but rather as an economic convenience for those of the higher castes. According to Gandhi, untouchability is a corruption, and thus he sought to bring a measure of equality to India, not by attacking Hindu traditions, but by revealing that the oldest and most authentic of those traditions do not fully sanction caste and do not, in the least, sanction untouchability.

Gandhi's campaign for universal equality was integral to the advancement of his campaign for a self-governing, independent India. The lessons this holds for you as a business leader have less to do with ethics—although Gandhi's example is surely relevant in this regard—than with ensuring that everyone with whom you do business—customers, staff, colleagues, subordinates, bosses, investors, and so on—is given a stake in your enterprise. That way, everyone will feel a commitment to you and your organization. Businesses do no business with other businesses; *people* do business with *people*. Treat everyone with respect, render everyone fair value for value received, and those people will return to you time and again. You will have made more than a sale; you will have created a customer, a client, a loyal employee, a committed colleague, a grateful boss, a confident investor. In essence, you will have created a partner in your success.

■

Lesson 20
RESPECT EVERYONE, ALWAYS

"In my opinion there is no such thing as inherited or acquired superiority. . . . I believe implicitly that all men are born equal."
~Speech at Tanjore, September 16, 1927

In Gandhi's India, whose Hindu majority had inherited a rigid caste system, the assertion of universal equality was a bold, jarring, even revolutionary act. Elsewhere, including in the United States, the assumption of equality was something virtually taken for granted—or such was the claim. Even today, however, universal equality is hardly universally accepted in the context of business. We typically treat bosses differently from subordinates, major customers (our "whales") differently from minor customers ("minnows"), key vendors differently from those we do business with only on occasion, and so on. This is neither necessarily aberrant policy nor bad policy. After all, at bottom, business is the exchange of value for value, and if one customer offers more value than another, it is a reasonable policy to treat that customer in ways that acknowledge what his business means to the firm. Yet, on the other hand, continually deciding who should get what kind of treatment is a time-consuming occupation that distracts you from matters more central to your business.

Much of what we do in business is analyzing, sorting, and classifying. It is very demanding work, and so it makes good common sense to apply the labor only where it is truly needed. In respect to your treatment of the various people with whom you do business, consider dispensing with at least some of the hard work of discrimination. Instead, assume universal equality and demonstrate the same respect for everyone with whom you interact. Not only will this policy of blanket respect put you on ethically unimpeachable grounds, but it will invite everyone to reciprocate. When a customer, client, boss, colleague, or subordinate receives from you greater value than might have been expected, the natural inclination will be to return to you greater value than originally might have been anticipated. In this way, the quality and value of every transaction across your business can be raised—and at no extra cost to your enterprise. In fact, quite the contrary: Whereas enhancing benefits delivered and received typically requires going the proverbial extra mile—that is, doing *more* work—treating everyone with respect all the time actually requires *less* work because you will no longer need to make an investment of resources in the demanding labor of analyzing, sorting, and classifying the "value" of each and every person you encounter.

■

Lesson 21
GIVE EVERY JOB A HIGH PROFILE

> "No one could uphold untouchability and still live in the Ashram."
>
> ~ "Removal of Untouchability," *History of the Satyagraha Ashram*,
> July 11, 1932

On May 25, 1915, Gandhi established an ashram—an independent, self-sufficient community—at the Kocharab bungalow of Jivanlal Desai, an Indian barrister and friend. On June 17, 1917, Gandhi moved the ashram to land on the banks of the Sabarmati River in Ahmedabad. Gandhi deemed this "the right place for our activities to carry on the search for truth and develop fearlessness, for on one side are the iron bolts of the foreigners, and on the other the thunderbolts of Mother Nature."

Among the many experiments in self-sufficient communal living that were carried out at the ashram, none was more important than the removal of the social, political, economic, and religious exile imposed upon the members of the lowest caste. Gandhi understood that achieving the embrace of the untouchables would require many of the faithful to make a virtually unthinkable change in their lives. Clearly, a step so profound and revolutionary as the removal of untouchability could not be accomplished on an exclusively ideological, theoretical, or even spiritual level. Gandhi needed for this to happen in the real world and accordingly devised a practical means of bringing it about.

As a class, the untouchables followed the lowest vocational callings, including those branded as "unclean." The members of the ashram pursued three of these: traditional loom weaving, hide tanning, and waste disposal. Moreover, they were not to be content with merely laboring in these areas but were also tasked with improving, wherever possible, the way these vocations were carried out.

Understandably, waste disposal was the most distasteful of the "untouchable" trades, but, working with an expert adviser, Gandhi devised various means to transform this labor into something more meaningful and ultimately life-giving. "Sanitary service," he wrote, "was looked upon not as a special calling, but a universal duty. No outside labour was engaged for this work." Waste ("night-soil") was buried in shallow trenches so that it was "converted into manure in only a few days." Gandhi had deliberately chosen for the ashram on the Sabarmati an apparently barren tract, so that he might demonstrate to the world how a collaborative community could produce fertility in even the most unpromising of places. Thanks to the method of waste disposal adopted at the ashram, the soil was "living up to a depth of twelve inches"—that is, rich and productive.

Unclean?

"Millions of bacteria are there to clean up dirt. Sunlight and air penetrate the ground to that depth. Therefore night-soil buried in the upper layer readily combines with the earth." Moreover, the "closets" (outhouses) were "so constructed that they are free from smell and there is no difficulty in cleaning them." At the ashram, the very quality of "uncleanness" was removed from this "unclean" activity, which was transformed from unspeakable labor performed by an untouchable class to a "universal duty" productive of life and purity, and therefore a joy and privilege to carry out.

It is the task of the leader of an enterprise to structure the organization in ways that honor the value of all the work that must be done. An effective manager ensures that each worker understands not just the assigned task, but what that task contributes to the greater "commonwealth"—i.e. the company. Moreover, the manager also promotes universal understanding and appreciation of every other worker's role. The mechanism of the organization is made utterly transparent and open to view. Everything that is done and everyone who works to do each job is given as high a profile as possible. The best-run companies are characterized by individual pride and satisfaction in doing excellent work toward common goals that pervade the entire organization.

■

Lesson 22
DEMONSTRATE YOUR WORTH

> "No one is high and no one is low in the world; therefore he who thinks he belongs to a high class is never high-class, and he who believes himself to be low is merely the victim of ignorance. He has been taught by his masters that he is low."
>
> ~ "Removal of Untouchability," *History of the Satyagraha Ashram,*
> July 11, 1932

A common error, Gandhi believed, was the confusion of social, economic, ethnic, and religious labels with what might be called one's core identity. The Brahmin, born into the highest caste of the traditional Hindu caste system, feels entitled to identify himself as a man of knowledge. "If a Brahmin has knowledge," Gandhi wrote, "those who are without it will respect him as a matter of course." In such an instance, the label and the reality will be perceived to coincide. "But if he is puffed up by the respect thus shown to him and imagines himself to belong to a high class, he directly ceases to be a Brahmin. Virtue will always command respect, but when the man of virtue thinks much of himself, his virtue ceases to have any significance in the world." As soon as the Brahmin relies on the label that has been applied to him, he no longer manifests knowledge and, in fact, reveals ignorance. His action is not that of a wise man, so he cannot be meaningfully identified as a Brahmin, the circumstances of his birth notwithstanding.

In business, brands are of great importance, whether you are selling soap or marketing yourself and your value to a customer or an employer. Esteemed brands of soap get that way, not because of their label, but because of a reputation for demonstrated excellence, which the label or brand merely represents. In much the same way, you build your personal brand by demonstrating excellence. The brand does not confer excellence on you, but rather serves to communicate to others your reputation for producing it. If you cannot earn a desirable identity through consistently high levels of performance, others will brand you—and the identity they confer will hardly be desirable.

Whatever else Gandhi's campaign to abandon caste was, it was a call for each person to strive to earn a worthwhile identity through hard work, noble service, and necessary sacrifice. These constitute virtue, and virtue, in turn, constitutes moral identity. This lesson applies in any field of endeavor.

■

Lesson 23
MAKE YOUR LEADERSHIP ORGANIC

"We have assumed that we can get men to do things by force and, therefore, we use force."

~ "Brute Force," *Hind Swaraj*, 1909

"If I cease stealing for fear of punishment," Gandhi reasoned, "I would recommence the operation as soon as the fear is withdrawn from me. This is almost a universal experience." Gandhi did not reject coercive change, including violent revolution, just because he considered it immoral–though he certainly did consider it such. More importantly, he rejected it because he was convinced that force was an ineffective means of motivating people to change. Force operates on the victim's fear that, if he refuses to do as he is told, painful force will be applied (or reapplied) to him. As a motivating factor, force is fueled by fear–specifically, a fear of something threatening pain from the outside. Because the coercive motivation is not internal or organic to the person who is motivated, it is inherently weak and fatally flawed. Remove the external source of fear, and the motive disappears. "Persuasion" by coercion requires the continual application of force in order for it to remain persuasive. It is like an insatiable beast. Deprived of the food it craves, it dies.

The most powerful motivation is self-sustaining and does not depend on the application of force from the outside. To move your organization in a given direction, it is always best to achieve buy-in from all the stakeholders in the enterprise. Prove that the change you want provides a benefit to them. Give them a stake in your goals. Make your leadership organic–meaningful and desired–for everyone you lead. Avoid threats. Avoid all motivational strategies that rely on fear, not just because coercion is morally bankrupt (which it is), but because it is unsustainable.

■

Lesson 24
YOUR COMPANY IS YOUR FAMILY

"Members of an institution should be regarded as a family."
~ "The Best Field for Ahimsa," *Harijan*, July 1940

Ahimsa, the doctrine of nonviolence, was a difficult policy to implement. Gandhi therefore presented it in the context of the family, albeit "in a wider sense than the ordinary." He advised his followers to regard any institution in which they were involved as a family. From this stage of thought, the next step was to regard the "whole world [as] one family." In this frame of mind, the person committed to nonviolence would "fear none, nor will others fear him."

Many business leaders shy away from thinking of the members of their "institution" as a family. Some resort to a vague commandment always to separate business from personal matters. Others fear being thought of as "paternalistic" (or "maternalistic"), while still others simply feel that the analogy between their relationship to their employees and their relationship to their family is contrived at best and utterly false at worst.

The fact is that any CEO who regards her business as a family in a literal sense is making a mistake. The relations between one's actual family and one's "family" of associates, colleagues, subordinates, and bosses are inherently different, if only because genetics and nurture, which create strong familial bonds, don't apply in a work context. Yet it is still possible, as Gandhi suggests, to regard the members of the enterprise as a family, in the sense that each member has his own life and his own role to play, yet all are united in a commonwealth. The concept of the enterprise as "a team" is too feeble to describe the nature of this relationship. In any business, the well-being, livelihood, and future of each member is dependent on the performance, behavior, caring, and good faith of all. Each member must take individual responsibility for doing his own job and playing his own role, but upon this independence a corporate interdependence is built. Beyond this, the family model is very effective for putting disputes and conflicts in perspective. Disagreement and debate are just as essential to the success of a family as they are to any other enterprise—provided that the disputes are conducted with the intention of improving the common endeavor rather than tearing the organization apart. Every family has its quarrels, but if the family is healthy and functioning well, the differences are always contained within the boundaries of the familial commonwealth.

In thinking about your organization, starting from the model of the family can be a helpful guide to point you in a productive direction. Focusing on this model, less with your head than with your heart, puts everyone in the state of interdependent independence that is optimal for the best performance an "institution" can achieve. Gandhi's admonition to regard all of your meaningful associations as your family was not so much a moral imperative as it was an organizational imperative. For him, the family analogy was the cardinal principle of group dynamics, the essential ingredient in the creation of a more successful "institution."

■

Lesson 25
GIVE UNCOMMON PEOPLE A COMMON IDENTITY

> "Let all of us consider that we are Shudras. Then there will be no feeling of high or low left."
> ~Answers to questions at Gandhi Seva Sangh meeting, May 6, 1939

In his campaign against the caste system, Gandhi proposed restructuring modern Indian society according to the more traditional class concept of *varnas*, as prescribed in Hindu scripture. The four traditional varnas are Brahmin (the class of scholars, teachers, law makers, and preachers), Kshatriya (members of the military and the secular ruling class), Vaishya (mainly merchants and dairy farmers), and Shudra (non-dairy farmers, craftspeople, and laborers). Having proposed a return to this earlier form of social structuring—in which there are classes, but no hard-and-fast restrictions regulating mobility or interaction among them—Gandhi then appealed to all of his followers simply to consider themselves Shudras, members of the lowest varna. "Then there will be no feeling of high or low left."

Gandhi did not ask anyone to abandon his trade or profession and become a farmer, an artisan, or a simple laborer, but he did ask that each Indian voluntarily class himself as one of this group. His object was to give everyone a common identity without forcing anyone into a single, uniform mold. In this request, Gandhi created an extraordinary lesson for anyone who is tasked with creating commitment and unity of purpose in an organization.

The last thing a competent CEO wants is a company consisting of yes-people who have identical skills and cookie-cutter thoughts. A carpenter would have little success in her work if nothing but hammers were to be found in her toolkit. A company achieves uncommon excellence by bringing together uncommon people for a common purpose. As Gandhi did, the leader of a company that aspires to excellence must find ways to give the members of his organization a common identity without sacrificing the unique talents, experience, and perspectives of individual employees. This requires setting forth clearly defined and significantly challenging goals of obvious high value, securing full organizational buy-in to these goals, and then giving the widest possible latitude to middle managers and their staffs to find or create the best routes to the goals. Effective management is a process of pulling together as well as letting go. But the release is meaningless if the members of the organization lack an understanding of and a dedication to their common objectives and goals.

■

Lesson 26
RECRUIT RESULTS, NOT PEOPLE

> "By patriotism, I mean the welfare of the whole people, and if I
> could secure it at the hands of the English, I should bow down my
> head to them. If any Englishman dedicated his life to securing the
> freedom of India, resisting tyranny and serving the land, I should
> welcome that Englishman as an Indian."
>
> ~"Italy and India," *Hind Swaraj*, 1909

The objective and the measure of effective leadership are results.
It follows, therefore, that a CEO should enlist personnel, not on
the basis of who they are, but on what results they can produce.
Gandhi was less interested in recruiting born Indians into the
service of the campaign for home rule than he was in gathering
any and all who dedicated themselves "to securing the freedom
of India, resisting tyranny and serving the land." By their manifest dedication—the results they aimed to achieve—such people
were functionally Indians, whether they hailed from London or
from Delhi.

The ability to "read" people is a formidable skill for any leader
or manager to possess, but a CEO is not a psychologist—nor should
she try to be. She reads people, not for the purpose of assessing
their whole personality or to cure them of some emotional afflic-
tion, but to predict the results they are likely to produce for the
organization she leads. Likely results, doubtless, are related to an
individual's official job description, demonstrated areas of
expertise and training, and, yes, visible aspects of personality. But
the savvy CEO understands that results are rarely simply and
absolutely determined (let alone guaranteed) by these things. In
some situations, for instance, a problem in the sales department is
more likely to be solved by someone in customer service than by
someone in sales. Focus on the results you need, *then* connect the
person to the results. If you have good reason to believe a customer

service staffer can productively dedicate himself to fixing the problems in sales, ignore his job description and welcome him as an expert in the field of selling.

Recruiting your teams and managers based on the results you need, rather than on the formal labels attached to personnel, demands sufficient imagination to see through categories to the objectives and goals you want the organization to attain. To be sure, it is quicker and easier to rely on labels—at least until you fail to obtain the best possible results. Both doing over and learning to live with something short of excellence are ultimately a lot harder than exercising intelligent, flexible imagination at the front end, the point in time at which you put together a work group.

■

Lesson 27
NEVER TURN YOUR BACK ON DISSENT

"Policy must always be decided by a majority vote, but it does not cancel the minority vote."

~ "Is Non-Violence Impossible?" *Harijanbandu*, August 10, 1940

In many companies, the only vote that counts in policy matters is that of the chairman, CEO, or owner. For all practical purposes, this single vote *is* the majority vote. Some leaders, having made their decision, turn their backs on those who express dissent. "It's my way or the highway," the macho maxim runs, and, depending on the nature of the enterprise, this may not be such a bad approach to management. Yet oftentimes it leaves a bad taste, both for the dissenting minority (which may, in fact, constitute the entire organization, save for the CEO, chairman, or owner) and for the person whose "vote" constituted the majority. Typically, doubt and discontent linger when the issues involved are significant matters of principle. To turn your back on principled dissent is to court any number of problems, ranging from loss of morale, to disloyalty, to unwanted staff turnover, to outright disaster.

Gandhi's life and life's work were built on the right and duty of dissent, and he never turned his back on it. The will of the majority, he held, must not cancel the vote of the minority; however, where "there is no principle involved and there is a programme to be carried out, the minority has got to follow the majority. But where there is a principle involved, the dissent stands, and it is bound to express itself in practice when the occasion arises."

Straightforward, unalloyed insubordination—an employee's refusal to perform the job for which he contracted or to carry out a task required by his job description—cannot be tolerated. But principled dissent—a disagreement that touches on long-standing company policy or issues of ethics—should neither be ignored nor punished. Principled dissent is always potentially valuable to the organization and should be heard and evaluated. Quite probably, the minority view will not alter the action on which the majority (even if this "majority" is no more or less than the person in charge) has decided. Nevertheless, minority dissent frequently provides a valuable additional perspective on the majority decision, suggests possible adverse consequences of the decision, and raises issues to be taken into account in the future. You cannot afford to discard, let alone penalize, any point of view that is developed and presented in good faith.

Each perspective on a decision enhances the decision, even if the perspective is one of critical dissent. Listening to, evaluating, and respecting dissent does not obligate the majority to yield to the minority. The weak CEO interprets dissent as a threat, when it is really a lesson, the gift and boon of additional data concerning a decision and an action that may be critical to the organization. In any collaborative endeavor, if everyone is thinking alike, no one is really thinking.

■

Lesson 28
INFLEXIBLE GOALS, FLEXIBLE METHODS

> "What does it matter that we take different roads so long as we reach the same goal?"
>
> ~ "The Condition of India (continued): The Hindus & the Mohomedans," *Hind Swaraj*, 1909

Gandhi's India was torn between Hindus and Muslims. This violently destructive religious conflict prevented Indians from uniting effectively in their mutual struggle for home rule against the British authorities. A profoundly religious man, Gandhi did not deny the importance of religion but defined all religions as "different roads converging to the same point." This being the case, he saw no reason for disputing their differing processes for reaching the same goal. "Wherein is the cause for quarreling?" he asked.

Seeking to effect change, Gandhi focused on ways to change outcomes rather than ways to change people. His approach is a valuable example for anyone whose job it is to lead an organization to change. Telling an account executive that he'd better develop a "selling personality" is far more likely to produce anxiety, disappointment, and resentment than it is to improve the sales department's quarter. On the other hand, analyzing the underperformer's *results* and setting reasonable goals for improving them offers a better chance for success. After all, straightforward, uncomplicated results are inherently more fixable than complex human beings.

The CEO cannot afford to neglect the human capital of the enterprise. Whether you make shoes or sell stocks, every business is first and foremost a people business. But the goal of managing human capital is not to change people; it is to guide and improve performance. It matters far less by what route an account executive hits or betters his numbers than that he manages to reach—or better—the prescribed benchmark.

[65]

Goals are goals. At any given time, they are absolute for a department or a company. In contrast, process and style are complicated functions of individual personality, attitude, strengths, and weaknesses. These factors may require analysis and modification, and they are appropriately the subjects of constructive criticism, but the most productive approach to leading toward improvement is to combine inflexibility where goals are concerned with substantial flexibility when it comes to the method and style used to reach them. Tolerate nothing less than excellence, but open the organization to the greatest possible tolerance for a range of personal processes that achieve excellence. To do otherwise is to become at best obstinate and at worst tyrannical.

■

Lesson 29
LEADERS NEVER FOLLOW

"The best men are supposed to be elected by the people."
~ "The Condition of England," *Hind Swaraj*, 1909

Like every nation, every business must successfully create the form and mechanisms of effective government. Those who see democracy as the ideal form of government believe that the people naturally tend to elect the best men to govern them. "But, as a matter of fact," Gandhi observed, "it is generally acknowledged that the members [of the British Parliament] are hypocritical and selfish. Each thinks of his own little interest. It is fear that is the guiding motive. What is done today may be undone tomorrow." Judging from the dismal public approval statistics that surround recent U.S. Congresses, Americans by and large share Gandhi's assessment of the quality of their elected representatives. Yet few Americans would willingly abandon the principle of democracy that asserts, "the best men are . . . elected by the people."

No democracy, including the American democracy, has ever satisfactorily addressed this spectacular instance of what psychologists call cognitive dissonance: the feeling of discomfort that arises when one experiences two contradictory thoughts simultaneously or attempts to adhere to mutually exclusive beliefs or values, as in the case of someone behaving in a way that contradicts his beliefs. But the failure of democracy to close the gap between values and behavior does not excuse you and your enterprise from both addressing and resolving such contradictions.

Gandhi believed the problem was that the British Parliament was "without a real master." As a democratic institution, Parliament was supposed to represent the people, but (in Gandhi's view) it rarely did. Yet even if it did fulfill its mandate, what, finally, did it mean to "represent the people"? Gandhi believed that the "people change their views frequently," making it impossible to achieve "finality" in the work of Parliament.

Let's leave aside the thorny problems of national government and return to the issues of entrepreneurial leadership. It is the first task of a CEO to determine who his "real master" is. Is his function to represent his employees? His shareholders? His clients and customers? The needs and wants of these three groups do not typically coincide. Employees want higher salaries, shareholders want lower costs and higher profits, while customers want the best value—high quality at a low price. Moreover, is the customer always right? Or the employee? Or the shareholder? Does merely representing their interests (were this even possible) constitute true leadership?

The way out of this thicket—a swamp without firm ground—is to discover, evolve, define, and embrace values that encompass yet transcend all of the individuals who hold a stake in the company. These values must be as final and unchanging as anything that changeable people can produce. They must function as the "laws" of the company "government" and, as such, must be taken collectively as the "master" that the CEO properly serves. If he fails in following these master principles, he will soon find himself following those whom he is supposed to lead. And who would call that leadership?

■

Lesson 30
RECONCILE THE IRRECONCILABLE

> "The capitalist is as much a neighbor of the labourer as the latter
> is a neighbor of the former, and one has to seek and win the
> willing co-operation of the other."
> ~ Speech at meeting of village workers, Nagpur, February 23, 1935

Gandhi built perhaps the most momentous social movement of the twentieth century on breaking the law—when the law was wrong. But not every law that merits breaking is to be found on the statute books.

That the capitalist is the irreconcilable enemy of the laborer, and vice versa, has been taken as a virtual law of nature at least since the work of Marx and Engels. In addressing workers in an Indian village during a labor action, Gandhi acknowledged a "conflict of interest between capital and labour," but he went on to point out that the two groups live in the same world and even in the same community. They are neighbors and, as such, are obliged to find a means of breaking the "natural" law that defines capital and labor as enemies. Acting on the basis of their situation as neighbors, they need to find a way of working in willing cooperation for the benefit of both.

Like America's Franklin D. Roosevelt during the Great Depression, Gandhi strove to bring economic enemies together by educating them to the fact that each needed the other. The capitalist needed labor, and labor needed the capitalist. Thus, he described the relationship, not as one of enmity, but rather as one of symbiosis:

interdependence for mutual benefit. Having recast the relationship between labor and capital, Gandhi found it necessary to break Marx's and Engels's "law" of nature in order to foster an environment of peace and mutual cooperation.

Leading an enterprise often calls for the reconciliation of apparently irreconcilable differences. Attempting to minimize or deny the conflict at hand is a resolution strategy that is doomed to fail. Alternatively, compelling one side to yield to the other is certainly not a viable long-term solution. Therefore, one is left to search for a new definition of the terms of the conflict—one that stakes out the common ground instead of dwelling on the disputed territory. Sometimes this can be achieved by reapportioning work assignments and resources. Sometimes all that is required is to demonstrate that what appears to be a legitimate cause of conflict is really an even more legitimate cause for cooperation. Whatever the route to resolution, converting relationships of enmity into relationships of cooperation requires both sides to see themselves as standing to make significant gains.

Lesson 31
LEAD TOWARD ENLIGHTENED ANARCHY

> ". . . Thoreau has said . . . that that government is best which
> governs the least."
> ~ "Enlightened Anarchy—A Political Ideal," *Sarvodaya*, January 1939

In January 1939, with the planet on the verge of a second world war, Gandhi reflected that "political power" could not be the "ultimate aim" of India's independence movement. Defining political power as the "power to control national life through national representatives," Gandhi went on to observe that these representatives would "become unnecessary if the national life becomes so perfect as to be self-controlled." His ideal government was an "enlightened anarchy in which each person will become his own ruler" and will "conduct himself in such a way that his behavior will not hamper the well-being of his neighbours."

Gandhi's followers addressed him as "bapu" (father). Superficially regarded, this epithet suggested total devotion, a complete investment of authority in one figure—the very opposite of enlightened anarchy. Yet, if we follow the parental analogy through, we see that the leadership model "bapu" implies is, in fact, leadership toward a government in which each person becomes his own ruler. After all, the mission of any parent is to lead his or her children toward self-government: a life without parents.

The ideal toward which any CEO should lead his company is a productive, profitable existence without him and, indeed, without any central authority. This does not mean that a CEO should work toward his own elimination, nor does it mean that the company should actually be run without a CEO and managers. What it *does* mean is that those in leadership positions should make it their mission to create an enterprise whose members are capable of self-government in the highest possible degree. An attitude of enlightened anarchy enlivens any collective endeavor, even if it remains an idea, an ideal deliberately left unrealized. Promote the independence and autonomy of each member of the organization, and you will create an enterprise in which cooperation and collaboration are voluntary—in the deepest sense, self-motivated, virtually reflexive in nature. Ten minds following the same pattern, thinking the same way, are no more powerful than a single mind, but ten independent thinkers focused on a common goal are ten times more powerful.

A CEO's effectiveness can be measured by the degree to which she renders her presence optional to the organization. The best leaders lead to become unnecessary.

5

Learning and Experience

Gandhi put less stock in formal education than in learning from experience. From his legal training, he came to believe that lawyers function mainly to promote disputes rather than to settle them or to bring justice. Nevertheless, his *experience* as a lawyer taught him both the power and the weakness of the legal system and that leveraging a government's laws in nonviolent campaigns of civil disobedience could transform not just the government but society itself.

The lessons in this chapter identify Gandhi's use of study and experience as examples any leader can apply. Gandhi came to understand that education and experience could be both liberating and confining. For him, managing beneficial change depended on knowing what knowledge to use and what knowledge to look beyond, modify, or reject entirely.

Lesson 32
EXPERIENCE TRUMPS EDUCATION

"He had no education, save that of experience."

~ *An Autobiography*, 1948

Gandhi's father was not educated beyond the elementary grades and had nothing more than an education that gave him basic literacy. "Of history and geography he was innocent," Gandhi wrote. Nevertheless, he judged that his father's "rich experience of practical affairs" enabled him to solve "the most intricate questions" and prepared him to manage hundreds of men in business.

Our age is obsessed with diplomas and certificates. These, certainly, are of value. However, it is a big mistake to minimize the value of experience, which is a highly effective teacher—perhaps the best teacher of all. Even more, it is an act of arrogance to take the position that experience is no substitute for "formal" education in a given field. The fact is that experience is often superior to formal education.

In recruiting, hiring, and managing employees, look beyond the titles and papers that certify a given level of education and, instead, drill down into the candidate's or employee's practical experience. Explore it, exploit it, reward it.

■

Lesson 33

RELEVANT DECISIONS COME FROM RELEVANT EXPERIENCE

"For experience convinces me that permanent good can never be the outcome of untruth and violence."

~ "My Path," *Young India*, December 11, 1924

Lest we forget, one of the principal attributes of a CEO, the person "in charge," is experience. As a teacher, experience has no equal— although a great deal also depends on the receptivity of the student. Turn to your experience when you require an index against which to evaluate a proposed project, program, or course of action, and do not hesitate to identify and announce experience as the basis of your decision. Just be certain that your decision really is based on your thorough, honest evaluation of your relevant experience. As Gandhi has done here, use particular instances of experience as the foundation on which to build enduring rules, rules of thumb, principles, and articles of policy.

But beware. Apply the word *experience* indiscriminately, and you will soon find that you have squandered all of its value. As a leader, you cannot afford to create the perception that your experience is no more than a convenient way to settle an argument.

■

Lesson 34

ABSORB THE IDEAS YOU NEED

"I lay no claim to originality."

~ Preface, *Hind Swaraj*, 1909

Introducing his short book advocating and explaining *swaraj* for India, Gandhi did what few other authors would dare: He confessed to having no original ideas. "The views" in the book, he explained, "are mine, and yet not mine." They were formed "after reading several books," from which he absorbed ideas and made them "almost a part of [his] being." Moreover, he believed himself entitled to lay claim to the concepts he had so shamelessly appropriated because he hoped "to act according to them." Use an idea productively and in good faith, and it is yours.

Good ideas are everywhere, but many managers resist them for one reason and one reason only: *They* did not think of them. Management analysts sometimes call this attitude NIH (not invented here) syndrome.

Effective managers use whatever works for them. *Exceptionally* effective managers absorb what they find, making it their own. Instead of merely lifting, exploiting, and discarding an idea you encounter, try revolving it in your mind, so that you might examine it from every angle in search of more applications. A given idea may not be original with you, but if you create original applications for it, you can bring something new and powerful into the world.

It is not wrong to steal ideas; it is merely insufficient.

When you find something that excites you—a concept, a method, or a product that strikes you as having significant potential—don't just pocket it. Instead, swallow it; make it a part of you. It is almost impossible to overwork a good idea, but all too easy to overlook one.

■

Lesson 35
SPEAK THE LANGUAGE

> "I think that we have to improve all our languages."
>
> ~ "Education," *Hind Swaraj*, 1909

Gandhi taught that language was a powerful means of bonding people to one another as well as to authority. He believed that English was an important language, and he himself wrote extensively in it. Yet to the extent that Indians learned and communicated in English *instead of* the languages indigenous to India, they were bonded to the overlords instead of one another and were therefore in danger of becoming more English than Indian. Gandhi taught that the British authorities used English to enslave Indians, and therefore he prescribed education in one's own provincial language, plus Hindi, which he believed should be adopted as a universal language for India. In this way, language would serve India and Indians, not the British.

In order to enhance his awareness of the company's operations, clarify his expectations, and prevent costly miscommunications between departments, a CEO or manager must be able to communicate effectively in any of the specialized languages of his organization. When speaking with computer specialists, for instance, he should use and understand basic IT terminology; likewise, a grasp of basic marketing vocabulary prevents important information from being lost in translation when communicating with the marketing department. But among the most important tasks any leader undertakes is to ensure that everyone in the organization speaks the same language—that is, a language meaningful to the business of the enterprise and to its members. And the universal language in which everyone has to be fluent is the language of business itself. This language is called "money."

Money is the lingua franca, the Esperanto, the universal tongue of all enterprise. This does not mean that all communication must be a cash-only transaction, but it does require that whatever is said and written must finally be accountable in the quantifiable terms of assets spent and assets gained, of cost, profit, savings, loss, and value. Whatever the particular subject of a communication, it must ultimately be relatable (though not necessarily reducible) to the bottom line.

Oxygen alone is not sufficient to sustain life, but everyone requires oxygen in order to live. Money is the oxygen of enterprise, and it must therefore figure in everything that is done and said in business. Whatever specialized languages one uses—and a CEO must have a working knowledge of them all—the universal language of business is the language of money. The more fluently you speak it, the more compelling your message will be.

■

Lesson 36
THE LIMITS OF PRECEDENCE AND PROTOTYPE

"The people of Europe learn their lessons from the writings of the men of Greece or Rome, which exist no longer in their former glory."

~ "What Is True Civilization?" *Hind Swaraj*, 1909

Gandhi revered those who had come before, but he never slavishly followed precedent. One of the problems he saw in European civilization, especially with regard to the laws and morality it produced, was its having been founded on historical models long dead. In contrast, traditional Indian civilization was very much alive, a living legacy rather than a dead historical shell. Gandhi pointed out that Greece and Rome, upon whose legacy European civilization is based, "exist no longer in their former glory. In trying to learn from them, the Europeans imagine that they will avoid the mistakes of Greece and Rome. Such," he concluded, "is their pitiable condition."

The man or woman at the helm of any organization must endeavor to learn from the past but must never become wedded to it. Taken as a playbook, a source of predictive guidance and inspiration, the legacy of your enterprise is valuable. Regarded as a set of inviolable commandments, it is a dead hand—at best a source of arbitrary limitation, at worst downright destructive. There is much wisdom in the record of the collective experience of the past, but you must always bear in mind that bygone decisions were made in response to a particular reality at a particular time. To the degree that your connection with the past energizes and inspires your leadership, legacy is valuable; to the degree that you feel its force as a restraint, legacy threatens to put your organization in a "pitiable condition." Accept the past as a teacher, but remember that the measure of a successful teacher is the number of students who rise above his example, and the very greatest teachers are those who produce students much greater than themselves.

An ambition to repeat the past—to be equal to it—is "pitiable." The precedents of leaders who have gone before you should be steps you and your organization use to rise above them.

■

Lesson 37
ABANDON "FOOLISH" CONSISTENCY

> "[*Varna*] simply means . . . following . . . all the hereditary and traditional calling of our forefathers, in so far as that traditional calling is not inconsistent with fundamental ethics, and this only for the purpose of earning one's living."
> ~Speech at Trivandrum, October 10, 1927

To engineer change in any organization is actually a balancing act that straddles the status quo and innovation. Attempting a sweeping, one-step transformation is a daunting prospect with the odds stacked against it. Forcing people to throw out tradition and comfortable habit is bound to create resistance. Gandhi, whose program of transformation was both sweeping and profound, revealed himself as a master manager of change, a thinker possessed of the ability to blend tradition and innovation in remarkable ways.

One of the great evils Gandhi sought to purge from India was the rigid caste system, which exiled many "untouchable" members of Indian society as it elevated the Brahmins above everyone else. Politically, economically, and religiously (for caste was part of Hindu belief), many Indians had made a heavy investment in the caste system and would not readily abandon it. Gandhi set about breaking through to these people by examining *varna*, the Hindu concept on which caste was based. He began by defining varna as an imperative to follow the calling of one's forefathers. Even the most conservative Hindu would not disagree with this. But then he went on to modify the scope of the imperative:

- One should follow the ancestral calling, but only "in so far as that traditional calling is not inconsistent with fundamental ethics."

- The imperative to emulate the ancestors is strictly vocational in its application, extending only to "the purpose of earning one's living."

The first part of the definition bowed to cherished tradition, whereas Gandhi's innovative modifications harmonized tradition with the call to equality. Whereas the traditional view of varna reinforced caste—strict and immutable social stratification—Gandhi's two modifications sought to make possible liberation from the system's hopeless constraints. The implication of the first modification was that varna must stop where fundamental ethics begins— that is, it must not be used to justify, let alone mandate, the continuation of the caste system. The second modification limited application of varna to the vocational realm, thereby implying that the force of varna did not extend to the larger control of social structure, personal conduct, and individual opportunity.

Gandhi's virtuoso reconciliation of tradition with change in the case of varna calls to mind a famous saying by one of his favorite American authors, Ralph Waldo Emerson. "A foolish consistency," Emerson wrote, "is the hobgoblin of little minds." Emerson did not scorn consistency, but only *foolish* consistency—consistency for consistency's sake, consistency that serves no rational and valuable purpose. Gandhi's appeal for change was to retain consistency— tradition—but only insofar as it was not foolish, a destructive drag on the present and future. Just as he refused to adhere to a foolish consistency, so he rejected rushing to a foolish innovation: the wholesale rejection of varna, which he regarded as an appropriately cherished aspect of Hindu social culture. Instead, he found a way of setting into motion the change he wanted: abandonment of the caste system, at least insofar as it raised some while lowering others.

Constructive change within an organization requires a managed revolution, one that identifies what needs to be changed and that separates it from what can and should remain relatively untouched, then executes a program of change designed to bring the best products of innovation while preserving the best aspects of the status quo. Contrary to what many a CEO believes, "shaking things up" is not a good end in and of itself. To be sure, even beneficial, positive change typically brings some temporary instability, and the less the better. As the leader of an enterprise, it is your job to make change simultaneously as meaningful and as seamlessly painless as possible. For all that he demanded of his followers, this, too, was Gandhi's aim. He sought to make great change, but with the least possible violence.

■

Lesson 38

NEVER SURRENDER TO MERE ORTHODOXY

"The interpretation of accepted [religious] texts has undergone evolution, and is capable of indefinite evolution, even as the human intellect and heart are."

~ "Caste Has to Go," *Harijan*, November 16, 1935

The strict social stratification of Hindu India was sanctioned by the *Shastras*, or Hindu scripture. By the mid 1930s, Gandhi had decided that caste was so fundamentally unjust and so destructive to the future of India that its ultimate justification in religious belief had to be attacked. He would not allow orthodoxy to trump human rights. Nevertheless, as we saw in the preceding lesson, he approached both the Shastras and religious belief with respect.

The least effective way to escape the negative effects of unquestioning belief—in other words, uncritical orthodoxy—is to attack it from the outside. It is far more effective to identify and exploit internal weaknesses within the body of orthodox belief. Gandhi, for example, argued that the Vedas, the most ancient of Hindu holy writings, supported "absolute equality of status." He further expressed his opinion that the Shastras were not uniformly a "revelation" and that, in fact, they had long been subject to many different interpretations, which he called an "evolution" reflective of evolution in the thought and sentiment of those who earnestly study the Shastras. He also asserted the superiority of moral sense and reason over any literal interpretation of the text of the Shastras. Finally, he pointed out that even those who look to scripture to justify the continued existence of the caste system cannot find anything in the holy texts that sanctions untouchability, the relegation of the lowest caste to unclean labor and a kind of internal exile within Indian society.

Like nature itself, belief abhors a vacuum. Once orthodoxy has been successfully undermined, you must fill the resulting void with a persuasive presentation of the ideas and policies you wish to promote. But even the first phase of introducing a new way of doing things—the act of overturning unquestioning belief—is in itself of great value. Gandhi would have enthusiastically agreed with the Apostle Paul, "The letter killeth, but the spirit giveth life." Living, and therefore evolving, thought—which changes in response to a changing reality—must never surrender to words embalmed on a page.

■

Lesson 39
IF YOUR MIND NEEDS CHANGING, CHANGE YOUR MIND

"I have never made a fetish of consistency."
— "Introduction to 'Varnavyavastha,'" *Harijanbandhu,*
September 23, 1934

Follow any political campaign and, sooner or later, you will hear one candidate accuse the other of "flip-flopping on his position." In other words, he is being accused of changing his mind—as if that were a bad thing.

In the introduction to a 1934 collection of his writings relating to the Hindu caste system and the campaign for Indian equality, Gandhi invited the reader to embrace his changing mind and accept the evolution of his thought: "I am a votary of truth and I must say what I feel and think at a given moment . . . without regard to what I may have said before on it." In fact, Gandhi went a step further, advising the reader to resolve any contradictions found between his earlier and his later writings by discarding the older work "without hesitation." "I do not claim omniscience. I claim to be a votary of truth and to follow to the best of my ability what seems to be the truth at a given time. As my vision gets clearer, my views must grow clearer with daily practice."

We prize consistency in our leaders, but to value this above truth itself is simply foolish. Scientists make new discoveries all the time and therefore change their theories concerning the nature of life and other phenomena of the physical universe. Why, then, should a CEO hold herself hostage to everything she thought or said in the past? CEOs, like scientists, make discoveries that change their approach to what they do.

So, how can self-consistency ever be allowed to trump the evolution of one's thinking or even of truth itself? Far better to exercise the courage to absorb a charge or two of "flip-flopping" than it is to ignore new knowledge and better ways of solving problems and achieving goals for the good of the common endeavor. Far better to take the heat than to give up learning.

■

Lesson 40
YOU *WILL* OUTLIVE YOUR ERRORS

"I may be unconsciously led astray for a while but not for all time."
~ "My Path," *Young India*, December 11, 1924

Most business leaders grow accustomed to thinking of time as an implacable enemy. Like so much else we reflexively believe, this is—at best—a half-truth. In fact, time is also an ally. Time does not stop when you make a mistake, even if it appears that way. If you are mistaken or misled, find the time to correct your course. The percentage of errors that are truly catastrophic—that is, long-lasting in their results—is vanishingly small. The vast majority are not only correctable, but, when interpreted in the context of time, are positive opportunities to learn and therefore to build better than before. Look, listen, learn, move on, live on, create anew, and improve. No error need be forever.

6

Making It Real

Gandhi passionately rejected what he deemed the unthinking assumption that idealism and realism were incompatible. He did not divide the universe into an ideal realm and a material realm, but rather saw the ideal as integral to reality. He knew from both history and experience that idealism could shape the "real" world and that no desirable reality was possible without an ideal conception of what it should be.

Just as idealism could be injected into the world as it really was, so that world needed to permeate even the loftiest of ideals. When the nineteenth-century Scottish essayist, historian, and philosopher Thomas Carlyle read that the American Transcendentalist writer Margaret Fuller had declared, "I accept the universe," he reportedly remarked, "Gad! She'd better." But for the dialect, it was something Gandhi might have said as well. He approached the world determined to engage it, to shape it, even to transform it. But to do this Gandhi knew that he had to "accept the universe," to recognize and understand the reality before him, to question it—by all means—but never to ignore or deny it.

The lessons in this chapter concern the accurate assessment and productive engagement of the realities that confront your organization, with an eye toward managing them for the best outcomes possible.

■

Lesson 41

PESSIMISM IS SELF-FULFILLING

"Hundreds of nations live in peace. History does not and cannot take note of this fact."

~ "Passive Resistance," *Hind Swaraj*, 1909

There is an old saying among newspaper editors: "If it bleeds, it leads." Bad news is not just bad news; for all practical purposes, it is *news*, period. What Gandhi variously called "truth-force," "soul-force," and the "force of love" was responsible, he said, for dissolving the "little quarrels of millions of families in their daily lives" as well as the peaceful existence of hundreds of nations. We don't hear of this because this is the normal condition of life, and history does not take note of the ordinary and the normal. "History is really a record of every interruption of the even working of the force of love or of the soul," Gandhi wrote. "Two brothers quarrel; one of them repents and re-awakens the love that was lying dormant in him; the two again begin to live in peace; nobody takes any note of this." However, if the two instead fall to shooting at one another, "their doings would be immediately noticed in the Press."

Our experience of the world naturally skews toward pessimism. The peaceful, productive, smooth running of any social mechanism, whether it is a government, a corporation, or a particular department in a particular office, makes no impression on history. Since there can be no such thing as unrecorded history—for history is, by definition, a record—the normal and the usual pass through us as if they did not exist. The abnormal and the unusual—the violent outburst, the failure of the "Big Deal" to come to fruition—are, in contrast, news: the stuff of record. The exceptions thus overshadow the rules in our view of much of our collective social and commercial experience.

Too many CEOs confound "pessimism" with "realism." Not only are they not one and the same, there is good evidence, based on Gandhi's insightful analysis of the inherently exceptional content of history, that pessimism and realism are very nearly opposites, and optimism, though certainly not synonymous with realism, is actually a closer approach than pessimism to an accurate view of the world.

Pessimism is depressing, but it is also strangely comforting because it so lowers our expectations that we are put in a position to avoid the painful shock of disappointment, should we experience failure. But pessimism also discourages innovation, imagination, vision, and even prudent risk-taking; in other words, it militates against everything that goes into any successful enterprise. For this reason, pessimism, though only at best a marginally accurate worldview, often seems unfailingly valid. By discouraging good business practices, the pessimistic prophecy is self-fulfilling.

Lesson 42
NEVER STAND STILL

> "Nothing in this world is static, everything is kinetic. If there is no progression, then there is inevitable retrogression."
> ~ "Is Non-Violence Impossible?" *Harijanbandhu*, August 10, 1940

The popular image of Gandhi's spiritualism is of a quest for peace, for a moral still-point in a frenetic world. The reality of Gandhi is far from this. He was an activist in every sense of the word. He traveled widely to explain and to persuade, to win India and the world to the idea of independence based on nonviolence. For him, there was no such thing as a settled question. Attaining and maintaining a principled life required continual intellectual progress and spiritual evolution. To rest on this journey was to drift. Either you moved forward through an effort of informed will or you were carried backward in an "inevitable retrogression" that threatened to undo all that you had gained.

Gandhi's vision of human interaction was kinetic. For him, life was a continuous series of transactions, each transaction creating a new reality that necessitated further transactions. Adherence to worthy principles gave direction to the movement, keeping it purposeful and positive while preventing it from drifting or becoming aimlessly frenetic, but principle neither created nor permitted stasis.

No enterprise ever simply arrives at its goal as a ship arrives at its dock. The idea of "maintaining" an organization's status is an illusion. It cannot be done. There is, as Gandhi explained, always movement, always change. The great leadership issue, therefore, is one of navigation: the creation of purposeful, productive movement within an environment of movement. This requires continual vigilance and planning as well as a high level of energy. Gandhi embraced these requirements of leadership, from which, in any case, he saw no escape. "Happiest are those that plunge in the fire," he wrote, citing the words of a traditional Indian poet. "The lookers-on are all but scorched by flames." Either enter the fray, thrusting and parrying, or stand still and be consumed.

■

Lesson 43
NEVER SWAP REAL VALUES FOR APPARENT GAINS

"The present peace is only nominal, for by it we have become emasculated and cowardly."

~ "The Condition of India," *Hind Swaraj*, 1909

Some Indians resisted Gandhi's call for home rule and independence by citing the so-called Pax Britannica—the peace brought to India by British rule, including protection from such indigenous terrorist tribes as the Thugs, Pindaris, and Bhils. To this argument, Gandhi responded that the bargain was a bad one. The price of this "peace" was forfeiture of Indian sovereignty and self-respect.

"A people who seek to exchange liberty for security deserve neither," Benjamin Franklin reputedly declared. The point both he and Gandhi made was the folly of trading a real and enduring value for an apparent and fleeting benefit. This is the great danger of compromising guiding principles, whether personal or corporate, in order to achieve some "pragmatic" end. Invariably, the immediate objective has a limited life, yet it has been acquired at the cost of something deep, valuable, and enduring. Unfortunately, the benefits of a bad bargain are exhausted far sooner than the harm that the bargain causes. Even if the damage, once recognized, can be controlled and possibly reversed, opportunities are lost, and the future has been made less secure by the sacrifice of real values for "nominal" gains. Greed, fear, and indolence are the three drivers of such bad bargains, and it is up to the CEO, as steward of the organization's values, to prevent anyone in the enterprise from succumbing to them—and thereby diminishing the enterprise as a whole.

■

Lesson 44
DEFINE YOUR PRESENT REALITY

> "I have no objection to your remaining in my country, but although you are the rulers, you will have to remain as servants of the people."
>
> ~ "Conclusion," *Hind Swaraj*, 1909

"Actions speak louder than words," we are told. Maybe louder, but not always more effectively. Gandhi used his entire being, his body and his life, to bring about change, but he also relied on words, using them so imaginatively that they prompted people to reassess and even redefine the various social, political, and economic relationships they had been taking for granted.

To India's English overlords, he proposed conceding that they were indeed the rulers of India. This was a fact. It would be ineffective—indeed, false—to deny it. But, having conceded this fact, Gandhi deftly redefined what it meant to be a leader—namely, to be a servant to the people one leads. "It is not we who have to do as you wish, but it is you who have to do as we wish." Having through words altered the perception of reality, Gandhi backed the words with proposed action. "If you act contrary to our will," he warned the British leaders, "we shall not help you; and without our help, we know that you cannot move one step forward."

Leadership is about accepting as well as changing reality; it is never about denying reality. The most meaningful and durable alterations to reality are made, not by force or imposition, but from within. This requires shaping and reshaping the perceptions and values of the people you lead. Sometimes these changes are best brought about by actions, sometimes by words, and sometimes—most of the time—by a combination of both approaches. Define the reality you want. Then determine what combination of acts *and* words will work most effectively to create that reality.

Typically, the most successful approach to change is to meet the status quo half way, as Gandhi did in conceding that the British ruled India. That is, begin by embracing reality as it is, but then take the next step by adjusting the terms of that reality to suit your ends. Think of the reality in which you and your organization operate as modeling clay. As the sculptor shapes his clay, so can you shape and mold reality in many ways. The simultaneous acceptance of reality as it is *and* the near infinite malleability of that reality is a central but rarely explored lesson from the experience of Mohandas Gandhi, yet it applies in virtually any context in which change is contemplated.

■

Lesson 45
DEFINE THE CHANGE YOU WANT

"You want the tiger's nature, but not the tiger . . ."

~ "What Is Swaraj?" *Hind Swaraj*, 1909

In politics as in business, change is always seductive. Students of marketing and advertising have long pointed out that you can print on a product label only one word more powerful than "Free!" It is "New!"

As a social and political activist, Gandhi recognized, stirred, and exploited the perceived need for change among the people of India. He understood, however, that few Indians had actually defined the change they wanted. To be sure, they *thought* they had. The majority believed that the change they wanted was to have, as Gandhi put it, "our own flag . . . our [own] navy, . . . army, and we must have our own splendour, and then will India's voice ring through the world."

Conceding that this indeed *sounded* desirable, Gandhi pointed out that these things meant that "we want English rule without the Englishman. . . . the tiger's nature, but not the tiger." Most Indians conceived of change as the eviction of the English people from

India but the retention of English principles, values, institutions, and cultural artifacts. They would, Gandhi protested, "make India English. And when it becomes English, it will be called not Hindustan, but *Englistan.*" This, he declared, was not the change he wanted. For him, true change—true *swaraj*, self-rule, independence—required a revaluation of values, not merely the eviction of the English followed by Indian reoccupation of their vacated shells.

Too often, CEOs define change as change in personnel—new blood. No doubt, such change is often necessary, but moving one manager out and another in does not of itself produce essential change. An organization should be more than the sum of its people, just as a viable government must be more than the sum of its leaders. John Adams, an architect of American independence and our second president, held above all else the objective of creating in the newborn United States a "government of laws, not men." Something very like this must be the aim of any enterprise that means to be sustainable over the long term, that hopes to outlive its founders. All of its leaders, managers, and employees must be faithful stewards of firm and fully articulated business principles, goals, and values. These may be superficially modified from time to time to adapt to changing markets—some may even be dropped and others added—but none of these changes can be the work of mere whim. If essential change is called for, that change must be made to the very value structure of the enterprise. It must be recognized as a profound and consequential action. It must be fully and thoroughly defined—defined, certainly, as something far more than the mere expectation that a new manager will, by virtue of being new, bring all the change the enterprise needs. As Gandhi well understood, true change is never so easy or so thoughtless.

■

Lesson 46
TRANSFORM A DISTANT GOAL INTO PRESENT OBJECTIVES

"The fact of the matter is that we do not know our distant goal. It will be determined not by our definitions but by our acts, voluntary and involuntary."

~ "Independence vs. Swaraj," *Young India,* January 12, 1928

Who could deny that goals—clearly defined, worthwhile, and ambitious—are essential to any business plan? Yet despite their obvious necessity, goals also have a downside. If the members of an enterprise focus narrowly on the goals of the organization—keep their eyes, as the saying goes, on the prize—there is a danger of stumbling in the present. The solution is certainly not to abolish goals, but to treat them in ways that don't attempt to clarify the future at the expense of policy and conduct in the present. Three leadership approaches can prevent the organization from falling into this trap.

First: *Break down goals into the objectives necessary to achieve them.* Gandhi frequently found himself obliged to counsel and preach patience. Many who demanded change were willing to accept as true change nothing less than instant and total change. Gandhi believed that this was not merely unlikely, but impossible. True change, as he understood it, works through the hearts and minds of people over time and therefore requires patience. Patience, however, does not mean inactivity. While the final goal might be distant in time, the steps toward it had to be completed as soon as possible.

In leading an organization toward a goal, the first step is to determine all the steps necessary to achieve the goal. These are the objectives, which, collectively, add up to a given goal. Once the objectives have been defined, the next leadership task is delegating the work to the right people and ensuring that they, you, and the rest of the organization have a clearly defined set of measures—metrics—by which each objective can be evaluated. In this way, the effort of the organization is focused on the present yet without losing awareness of the future.

Second: *Make goals present.* Most of us make the mistake of conceiving of a goal as something that does not yet exist, except in our imagination of the future. That is, we think of a goal as something that comes into existence only after it is achieved. This attitude is quite understandable. After all, if the goal you set for your company is to become the region's preeminent maker of widgets, you cannot say that you have reached your goal until the day you become the regional widget king.

At first glance, this seems not only self-evident but downright tautological: *You reach your goal only when you have reached your goal.* The problem with this kind of thinking is that it makes the verb (*reach*) inseparable from the noun (*goal*). When you are at the starting line of a race, you are obviously not at the finish line. This does not mean, however, that the finish line does not exist, whether you happen to be at the start of the race, or in the middle of the race, or actually crossing the line. For each runner, the finish line is always present, even though reaching it may be some distance off.

"If we are wise," Gandhi counseled, "we will take care of the present and the future will take care of itself." What he meant by this was to enfold the future into the present. Let the finish line inform the present hour—as well as the next, and the next.

Third: *Accept the dynamism of the goal.* Neither of the leadership principles we have just defined is complete. This does not mean they are invalid and should be discarded. Leaders need to set goals and break them down into constituent objectives. Leaders need to ensure that the goals of the enterprise inform everything the enterprise does from day to day. However, Gandhi recognized that goals are not necessarily absolutes. They are dynamic, "determined not by our definitions but by our acts."

For our purpose, which is to learn from Gandhi as an entrepreneurial leader and manager, we must assume that his own statement here is incomplete. It is true that the analogy between a goal and a finish line is not absolute. A finish line is definite, no matter what each individual runner may do in the course of the race; the goal of an individual or an organization may change as a result of "acts" performed in the course of time. Nevertheless, it is overstating (or incompletely stating) the case if we define a goal as *determined* by our acts. More realistically, a goal is the product of definition *and* act. It is as if the runner, having reached the 100-yard finish line, feels a new inspiration and decides to run to the 300-yard line and call *that* his goal. Or perhaps a more evocative analogy would be the sculptor who sets out to portray his subject in a certain way but, as the clay takes shape under his fingers, departs from—modifies, embellishes, simplifies—his mental conception of the work.

Goals are crucial to an enterprise, but they must not be allowed to tyrannize the organization. You should not feel obliged to steal from the present in order to feed the future, but neither should you feel that you must starve the future by failing to set goals. Break goals down into achievable objectives hour by hour, day by day, month by month. Keep goals present in the organization, no matter how distant they may be. Treat goals as a dialogue between definition, and act by allowing them to develop dynamically over time.

■

Lesson 47
KNOW THE COST

> "Not having really ever tried it, everyone appeared to be cnamoured of it . . ."
> ~ "Civil Disobedience," *Young India*, August 4, 1921

By the early 1920s, Gandhi had surprisingly little trouble "selling" the idea of civil disobedience—the nonviolent refusal to obey unjust laws—to members of the All-India Congress Committee (AICC).

The idea was so novel, and Gandhi presented it so persuasively, that many members of the congress conceived a "mistaken belief in it as a sovereign remedy for our present-day ills."

Having persuaded so many of so much, Gandhi did what few salesmen are ever willing to do: He took pains to readjust expectations by explaining that civil disobedience was a process that would take time and, even more, would require great sacrifice. After all, governments do not simply bow to those who disobey them. They respond with arrest and punishment. It is only when these measures fail to extort obedience that civil disobedience becomes truly effective. But provoking such a failure requires great courage and strength of will on the part of each person who disobeys the law. The cost is high. "Our triumph," Gandhi wrote, "consists in thousands being led to the prisons like lambs to the slaughter-house. If the lambs of the world had been willingly led, they would have long ago saved themselves from the butcher's knife. Our triumph consists again in being imprisoned for no wrong whatsoever. The greater our innocence, the greater our strength and the swifter our victory."

To put the government in the position of punishing the innocent condemns the government, delivering against it a powerful blow. The only advantage the government has is the people's fear of jails. "If only our men and women welcome jails as health resorts, we will cease to worry about the dear ones put in jails which our countrymen in South Africa used to nickname His Majesty's Hotels." Overcome that fear, and the government has no real power. Yet Gandhi was intent on driving home the cost of reaching this point. It was possibly years of imprisonment, years of putting one's life and freedom entirely at the mercy of a hostile government.

To inspire your organization to great effort, you must ensure that you employ no deception, whether inadvertently or on purpose. Emphasize equally the benefits to be gained by a certain course, the feasibility of the course, and also—as accurately as possible—its cost.

On September 12, 1962, President John F. Kennedy spoke to an audience at Rice University in Houston and set as the goal of the national space program to "go to the moon," explaining that we "choose to go to the moon in this decade and do the other things, not because they are easy, but because they are hard, because that goal will serve to organize and measure the best of our energies and skills, because that challenge is one that we are willing to accept, one we are unwilling to postpone, and one which we intend to win, and the others, too." Like Gandhi, Kennedy understood that the loftier the goal, the greater the effort required to attain it. However, also like Gandhi, he knew that it is far easier to inspire a company or a nation to make a strenuous, painful, high-cost effort for a truly valuable goal than it is to coax people into devoting relatively modest effort to something easily attainable but of little value.

Assess costs honestly. Instead of trying to disguise difficulty and sacrifice, use these as the selling points of a truly worthwhile goal. Effort and sacrifice feel good when they are perceived as the necessary price of something of high and enduring value.

■

Lesson 48
LIBERATE THE POSSIBLE FROM THE PROBABLE

"To believe that what had not occurred in history will not occur at all is to argue disbelief in the dignity of man."
~ "How Can India Become Free?" *Hind Swaraj*, 1909

A competent CEO relies on two compasses to chart the course of the organization he leads: the best available data, and probability. Probability is based on what has happened before—the history of the organization or of similar enterprises. Data and probability are indispensable to navigation, but even the most useful tools can be harmful if they are employed incorrectly or at the expense of some other valuable tool. Competent CEOs rely on data and probability; the truly great CEOs add a third tool: possibility. This is what separates the run-of-the-mill leader from the visionary.

Gandhi proposed for his nation a revolution with an objective that struck many as strange. He believed it possible to create an India so thoroughly "Indianized" that only those willing to wholeheartedly embrace the Indian identity—the political, philosophical, moral, and cultural values of the nation—would voluntarily remain in India. The rest would, again voluntarily, leave.

To the objection that such a revolution was literally unheard of, that such change had "never occurred in history," Gandhi replied that it "behooves us to try what appeals to our reason" and to do so, we "need not . . . refer to the history of other countries."

By simple definition, the possible contains the probable and not vice versa. Therefore, to limit what is possible only to that which is probable reduces the potential of any endeavor by imposing a limitation that sacrifices the visionary. To sacrifice the visionary is to deny the possibility of true innovation and invention.

Like any other force, vision can and must be managed. Gandhi understood this implicitly when he urged his countrymen to "try" an idea that "appeals to our reason," even though it was unprecedented in history and, therefore, literally improbable. The word *try* was critical to his meaning. Gandhi did not advise going for broke by discarding everything and committing to his vision. All he urged was that his idea be given a trial. Either it would produce satisfactory results or it would not. If not, something else could be tried.

Managing the possible should never be a reckless wager, but rather a careful trial. Vision must be continually tested against reality. Such testing implies prudence and caution, both of which are appropriate when the stakes are high.

Neither the probable (historical precedent) nor the possible (the product of vision) comes with any guarantees, yet no responsible leader would thoughtlessly toss out probability because it fell short of certainty. Why, then, discard the possible for the same reason? It is the mark and the role of the visionary leader to liberate the possible from the probable by refusing to allow history to tyrannize the future.

■

Exemplary Miracles

Lawyers and judges turn to their law books, and theologians to the Holy Scriptures. For Gandhi, there was no higher authority, no greater source of revelation, than the lives and deeds of men and women. He looked to them for models of action and conduct, and, most of all, he offered his own example to India and the world as a model for leadership toward the creation of universal justice and the pursuit of truth, on which all justice rests.

CEOs and managers come into their jobs with title authority, the force founded on their official job descriptions. It is not an inconsiderable force but, even so, it pales beside the force of the example they set by their deeds and conduct. In turn, as the following lessons suggest, any leader can learn from examples—including, of course, the example of Gandhi himself. The revolution he wrought in India—a revolution that instructed the world—seems miraculous in its depth and scope, and yet it was certainly real.

What greater validation can there be for arming yourself with the most ambitious dreams than the miraculous example of Gandhi:

one little man who faced down an empire? The lessons in this chapter are all about rejecting precedent as a constraint on what is possible, and instead embracing precedent as a liberation from our sense of so-called realistic limits. The most effective business leaders seek out examples to inspire and empower, while rejecting anything less as inadequate cautionary fables.

■

Lesson 49
THE POWER OF ONE

> "History shows that all reforms have begun with one person."
> ~ "Satyagraha ~ Not Passive Resistance," September 2, 1917

"What is the good," many earnest people asked Gandhi, "of only one person opposing injustice; for he will be punished and destroyed, he will languish in prison or meet an untimely end through hanging." Gandhi pronounced this objection "not valid" and turned to history to show that "all reforms have begun with one person."

The fact is that everything begins with an idea, and only one entity in the world can originate an idea: a human being. Thus, far from being exceptional, change *must* begin with one person. This is the nature of any innovation. Innovation does not come into existence as a result of a mass movement. People do not suddenly and simultaneously have the same idea, on which they suddenly and simultaneously decide to collaborate. One person has an idea and takes it to others. This is the root and beginning of change.

We often speak of the power of an idea. In actuality, an idea has no power. The person who creates and communicates the idea is the real source of the power represented in the idea, a power that is multiplied as the idea spreads and expresses itself in some action or set of actions. At this point, once the idea has "caught on," its originator may well be forgotten, thereby leaving us with the illusion that power originates in an idea or in a mass movement, compared to which a single human being seems small and insignificant.

Savvy CEOs think of their employees as human capital, the greatest asset the enterprise possesses. The savviest CEOs further understand that this asset is very different from all others, in that human capital is not simply the sum of its constituents. Say your company has assets of thousands, or hundreds of thousands, or tens of millions of dollars. Take one or two dollars away, and, for all practical purposes, your assets remain undiminished. A dollar is of little value, whereas a million dollars is of great value. In the case of your firm's human capital, however, the loss of a single person can mean the loss of any number of ideas capable of transforming your company. Build, develop, and use your human capital one person at a time if you want to get the most out of this asset.

■

Lesson 50
BE A QUIET EXAMPLE

> "The most effective, quickest and the most unobtrusive way to destroy caste is for reformers to begin the practice with themselves and where necessary take the consequences of social boycott. The reform will not come by reviling the orthodox."
>
> ~ "Caste Has to Go," *Harijan*, November 16, 1935

To effect change, change yourself. Take, for example, Britain's King Edward VII. When the monarch grew portly, he began leaving the bottom button of his waistcoat unfastened. This anatomical expedient started a fashion. All over Europe and much of the world, men began wearing their vests with the bottom button unfastened. The king, of course, neither commanded nor advised adopting this style. As a leader, he was naturally emulated.

Promoting change by personal example is most effective when you confront a particularly entrenched practice. Gandhi understood that "reviling the orthodox" for their continued strict observance of rigid social caste would meet with nothing but hard and angry resistance. By contrast, an example of tolerance and social equality—even beginning with a single person—was likely to spawn more examples, which, taken together, would eventually constitute social change.

As a CEO, you know that you carry official authority, but you must also become aware of your moral authority, which—like it or not—puts you on display as a model against which others will measure their attitude, belief, and behavior. Be sure you use this moral force with as much planning, wisdom, and imagination as you use the authority that officially comes with your job.

■

Lesson 51
EARN YOUR STRIPES

". . . one does not become a Brahmin by calling oneself a Brahmin. Not until a man reveals in his life the attributes of a Brahmin can he deserve that name."

~ "Introduction to 'Varnavyavastha,'" *Harijanbandhu*,
September 23, 1934

According to Gandhi, you are what you do, and how you do it. You may be appointed CEO, but you *are* CEO by virtue of your actions, your behavior toward others, and your stewardship of those you lead. Perform at your best on Monday, and you are a CEO on Monday. Merely coast along on Tuesday, and you may still have your fine office and brass nameplate, but you are not a CEO on Tuesday. A leader earns his stripes every day. Stop earning them, and they become nothing more than an empty symbol, signifying nothing. All honor, credibility, and authority flow from the words and deeds you produce one day after another.

A pessimist will interpret this *truth*—for truth it is—as grim: Authority is inherently exhaustible, so striving to maintain it is, therefore, inherently exhausting. But why not take an optimistic point of view? If authority is exhaustible, it is also both fluid and renewable. Earning the power to lead refreshes that power, restores you, and reinvigorates your enterprise.

Lesson 52
BE AN OPEN BOOK

"I have no secret methods."

~ "My Path," *Young India*, December 11, 1924

The truest, most effective, and most enduring leadership is always on prominent display. Attempts at leading by means of secrecy result in behind the scenes manipulation—covert management, as it were—rather than genuine leadership. It is the difference between aspiring to inspire others to do great things and contenting yourself with playing the role of puppeteer—one who manipulates others to do all that mere marionettes are capable of. Act publicly when you can, and in private act as if you were in public. A closed book has little meaning and less value.

Lesson 53
OWN (DON'T RENT) YOUR BELIEFS

> "For me non-violence is a creed. I must act up to it whether I am
> alone or have companions."
>
> ~ "Both Happy and Unhappy," *Harijan,* June 29, 1940

Policy and belief made manifest in public behavior was a key engine of social change for Gandhi. Nevertheless, Gandhi regarded his nonviolent creed as integral with his being, whether he was in company with comrades or on his own. Even the most sincere among us show one face in public and another in private, but anyone who occupies a position of responsibility must own her beliefs, not just rent them for public occasions. The renters will sooner or later be found out and labeled for what they are: hypocrites. For a leader, no identity is more crippling than this.

Gandhi always sought to ensure that he was so thoroughly permeated by his own beliefs that it would be impossible for him to behave differently in public than in private. Such immersion is part of the discipline of an effective leader.

If a tree falls in the forest, the hoary epistemological conundrum goes, *and no one is there to hear it, does it make a sound?* If we translated this cliché into the terms of effective leadership, Gandhi would not only readily understand, but easily answer: *If I betray my principles in private and no one is there to see, are my principles still intact?*

No. They are not. The reason? There *was* a witness: you.

Consistency of leadership principles is vitally important to the enterprise, but it is also important for you, yourself—at all times and under all circumstances, public and private. Allowing two senses of self to develop within you, one for public use and the other manifested in private, presents the insidious danger of insincerity, which will inevitably compromise your ideal of leadership. Gandhi taught that leadership is not a title or an official position, but rather a way of life, and life is lived when you are in company as well as when you are in solitude.

Lesson 54
PROVIDE POSITIVE PRECEDENTS

> "The people should . . . be made familiar with instances of pure
> satyagraha . . ."
>
> ~ "Instructions to Volunteers," Satyagraha Camp, Nadiad,
> April 17, 1918

A centerpiece of Gandhi's campaign for Indian home rule (and, sub-
sequently, independence) on the basis of universal human rights
was *satyagraha*, which he most succinctly defined as "fighting oppression through voluntary suffering." He knew that, to most people, the
satyagraha concept would seem naively idealistic, or even beyond
the reach of ordinary men and women. For this reason, he advised
volunteers in the service of Indian home rule to present to the
people stories of historical figures from Hindu, Islamic, and
Western sources who exemplify satyagraha.

When your task is to lead people toward innovation, it is important to create meaningful links between past precedent and the new
and unfamiliar ideas you are promoting. The more concrete and
familiar the precedents, the better.

Marketing experts claim that nothing sells merchandise more effectively than slapping the word "New!" on the label. While this may be
true for canned cleanser or a box of snack crackers, it is not an effective
approach when the merchandise you offer is a new idea—especially
one that presents intellectual challenges, threatens cherished beliefs, or
seems poised to encroach on jealously guarded professional or vocational turf. Instead of emphasizing the break with the past, therefore,
show the continuity of evolutionary change. Convey the benefits of
the new idea without conceding or even suggesting that there will be
any truly significant loss in the abandonment of the old and comfortably familiar ideas. Gandhi's recommended tactic was to avoid delivering lectures on abstract principles, especially if these principles were
likely to come across as radical or strange. Instead, like the lawyer he

had been trained to be, Gandhi relied on examples drawn, not from intellect and imagination, but from the real world. Precedent often speaks more persuasively than mere proposals.

■

Lesson 55
BE A SYNECDOCHE

> "A drop of water must yield to the analyst the same results as a lakeful."
>
> ~ "Non-violence," *Young India*, March 9, 1922

The ancient Greeks and Romans were avid students of language, especially language as a vehicle of persuasion. The classical rhetoricians of these cultures worked hard to identify and classify the various figures of speech that, together, form the arsenal of compelling argument. Among these is the "synecdoche," a figure of speech in which a part of something is made to stand for the whole thing. A familiar example is from the Lord's Prayer. When one of the faithful asks, "Give us this day our daily bread," he's not asking God for a slice of rye but for all necessary physical sustenance—for which "daily bread" is a synecdoche, a part that represents the whole.

Gandhi considered a person's every word and every act a synecdoche of the whole person. For him, our values are reflected in everything we say or do. "The nature of my non-violence towards my brother cannot be different from that of my non-violence to the universe," Gandhi wrote, acknowledging that his nonviolence toward a relative was representative of his nonviolence toward all.

As a CEO, a manager, or a supervisor, you are on display. Each thing you do or say represents who you are and what you stand for. These, in turn, both embody and communicate the values of the organization, department, or work group that you lead. Always remember that no company ever does business with another company. Each transaction is an instance of John doing business with Jane. For John, Jane *is* the business. John's sense and evaluation of his experience with Jane—whether it is a two-minute phone call or a six-month consultancy—will constitute his sense and his evaluation of Jane's entire company. As Gandhi vividly put it, "A drop of water must yield to the analyst the same results as a lakeful." Acting as a synecdoche for an organization is an endeavor with the highest possible stakes.

■

8

The Nonviolent CEO

This book marks the first time anyone has tried to give Mohandas Gandhi a seat in the boardroom, but the circa fifth-century BCE Chinese general and military theorist Sun Tzu has been there and done that. Modern CEOs enjoy fancying themselves the equivalents of generals—but, then, so did Gandhi, who was keenly aware that he was leading people, armed only with their force of righteous will, to possible death. And those CEOs who read their Sun Tzu carefully will note that even he deemed the best course, the sweetest victory, to be that achieved without hurting anyone: "To win one hundred victories in one hundred battles is not the acme of skill. To subdue the enemy without fighting is the acme of skill."

From Gandhi's example of nonviolence, the modern CEO may learn to be more, not less, aggressive—that is, to go into action before a war begins, to attack (as Sun Tzu advised) not the enemy's army but the enemy's strategy, thereby gaining victory without inflicting damage that hurts everyone, attacker and defender alike. The problem with violence, as Gandhi saw it, is that it enslaves rather than liberates. Violence begets violence, so ends achieved through harmful means permanently bond any achievement to a future of violence. Those who see victory in terms of defeating someone else only create new enemies. "An eye for an eye," Gandhi reportedly observed, "makes the whole world blind." The lessons that follow are drawn from Gandhi's aggressive campaigns of non-violent change.

■

Lesson 56
DISENGAGE FROM YOUR ADVERSARIES

"The force of arms is powerless when matched against the force of love or the soul."

~ "Brute Force," *Hind Swaraj*, 1909

Nothing relating to the teachings of Mohandas Gandhi is more familiar and more misunderstood than the doctrine of so-called passive resistance. In fact, as Gandhi practiced it, there is nothing at all passive about passive resistance, which, he explained, was more accurately called "love-force" or "soul-force."

By definition, a force cannot be passive. However, as Gandhi reasoned, people and groups may use two types of force in an effort to obtain what they want. "'We shall hurt you if you do not give this' is one kind of force," and the other "can thus be stated: 'If you do not concede our demand, we shall be no longer your petitioners. You can govern us only so long as we remain the governed; we shall no longer have any dealings with you.'" Gandhi also called this latter type of force the doctrine of "non-cooperation." The nonviolent removal of oneself from the equation of governor and governed is a manifestation of love-force or soul-force, more popularly but less accurately labeled passive resistance.

But how can a CEO use passive resistance? On the face of it, the proposition seems either oxymoronic or simply meaningless. The job of a CEO, after all, is to assert and exercise authority, not to resist the authority of others.

The truth is that any bid a CEO or other manager makes to assert authority invites a challenge to that authority. Too often, the result is the proverbial (if crudely expressed) pissing contest, the results of which range from useless, to wasteful of resources, to downright destructive. As in any auction, rival bids for authority raise the price of authority. There comes a time when the wisest course is to remove oneself from the futile contest. If, for example, Joe resists taking on an assignment, don't make it an order or otherwise browbeat him into accepting it. Instead, move on to Jill—and be sure to present the assignment to her as a great opportunity. Decline to cooperate with Joe. Decline to make his refusal powerful by disengaging from him and moving on to someone else. If you are in an aggressive frame of mind, you may think of this maneuver as cutting Joe off at the knees, but it is, in fact, an act of mentoring. You are teaching Joe to focus on the mission and not on the authority figures surrounding the mission. You are also teaching him not to pass up an opportunity when he is next presented with one. If you derive some satisfaction in thinking that you have cut off an adversary at the knees, well, it is only human to feel this way. But think beyond the image: Who wants an employee who has been cut off at the knees? A well-educated employee, by contrast, is always an asset.

■

Lesson 57
SOW AGGRESSION, AND AGGRESSION YOU WILL REAP

"You have disturbed your own peace; you are in perpetual fear..."
~ "Brute Force," *Hind Swaraj*, 1909

"Do no harm" is a familiar precept of the classical Hippocratic Oath once traditionally administered to all new physicians. Those who lead people in any enterprise would do well to borrow the precept as well as ponder it. Gandhi, who sought change on the most basic and sweeping of levels, embraced the spirit of this maxim. He explained himself by means of a hypothetical tale.

Suppose, he began, that a well-armed thief has stolen your property. His act enrages you, and "you argue that you want to punish that rogue, not for your own sake, but for the good of your neighbours." Toward this end, you gather a posse with the intention of taking his house by force. The thief hears of this and flees, but, now as angry as you, he assembles his own gang. He begins to prey upon the very neighbors on whose behalf you claimed to be acting. When they complain to you, you explain that "you are doing it all for their sake, you do not mind if your own goods have been stolen." The neighbors reply that "the robber never pestered them before, and that he committed his depredations only after you declared hostilities against him." Feeling bad for your neighbors, you nevertheless believe it impossible to back down without suffering disgrace. "Never mind," you tell your neighbors. "Come, my wealth is yours, I will give you arms, I will teach you how to use them; you should belabor the rogue; don't you leave him alone." This series of decisions, Gandhi explained, only leads to an escalation in violence: "And so the battle grows; the robbers increase in numbers; your neighbours have deliberately put themselves to inconvenience. Thus the result of wanting to take revenge upon the robber is that you have disturbed your own peace, you are in

[112]

perpetual fear of being robbed and assaulted, your courage has given place to cowardice."

It can be a most difficult mission to intervene in a dispute without exacerbating it. The more personally you intervene, the greater the chance that you will make things worse. Focusing on personalities and character can produce explosive results that only serve to escalate a conflict. In Gandhi's example, the man who claims to act on behalf of his neighbors really acts from motives of vengeance—albeit in the mistaken belief that the vengeance he seeks is also on behalf of his neighbors. By exercising brute force, he reduces himself to a brutish level of powerlessness. The more productive approach, Gandhi proposes, is to focus on what motivates the man's thievery rather than the fact that he is a thief. He advises turning from personality and character to motivating factors.

> You think that this stealing habit must be a disease with him. Henceforth, you, therefore, keep your doors and windows open, you change your sleeping-place, and you keep your things in a manner most accessible to him. The robber comes again and is confused as all this is new to him; nevertheless, he takes away your things. But his mind is agitated. He enquires about you in the village, he comes to learn about your broad and loving heart, he repents, he begs your pardon, returns you your things, and leaves off the stealing habit.

Any approach to change that involves aggression or coercion tends to escalate rather than reduce conflict. Sow brute force, and brute force you will reap. To avoid escalation and bring about amelioration, begin by making an effort to understand the motives behind the behavior you wish to change. Once you achieve this understanding, devise some way to alter or remove the motivations behind the acts and behavior you find objectionable and to substitute motivations that guide people in the direction you want them to go. It is far easier to analyze and alter motives than it is to attack or attempt to modify personality and character.

Instead of drawing a line in the sand and thereby inviting defiance, remove the motives for defiance. Your goal is not to defeat others, but to reposition them so that you—and they—can win. A spirit of collaborative commitment is far more sustainable than a mindset bent on grudging obedience. The former is a human capital asset, the latter a liability—and a liability that almost always becomes heavier with the passage of time.

■

Lesson 58
CHOOSE YOUR BATTLEGROUND

> "The English are splendidly armed; that does not frighten me, but it is clear that, to pit ourselves against them in arms, thousands of Indians must be armed."
>
> ~ "Italy and India," *Hind Swaraj*, 1909

During the long struggle for Indian home rule and independence, some cited the nineteenth-century example of the struggle of Italian patriots to unite the disparate duchies, principalities, and kingdoms on the Italian peninsula into a single Italian nation, free from the domination of Austria and other imperial powers. Gandhi believed the comparison was false. "India," he wrote, "can fight like Italy only when she had arms." If it were even possible to arm the nation, "how many years will it take?" he asked. More important, "to arm India on a large scale is to Europeanize it. Then her condition will be just as pitiable as that of Europe." The strategy would be quite literally self-defeating, since arming India would mean, "in short, that we must accept European civilization, and if that is what we want, the best thing is that we have among us those who are so well trained in that civilization. We will then fight for a few rights, will get what we can and so pass our days."

The most successful generals are those who never allow the enemy to select the battlefield. To do so yields a significant advantage, often both strategically and tactically. Similarly, the most successful CEOs never allow their company to be forced to compete on someone else's terms. The surest way to win is to play to your strengths. The surest way to lose is to play to the strengths of your competition. The strength of the British Empire was its armed might. To compete with it in this arena was to lose, either by suffering defeat by English arms or by surrendering Indian values to imitate European values, including the emulation of armed might. To fight a battle on the terms dictated by the enemy is to surrender before the contest even begins.

Fail to define your own identity, and someone will define it for you. This is true for individuals as well as for great corporations, in any competitive business. Know your strengths and make yourself competitive in the areas to which they apply. Do not allow yourself or your enterprise to be lured into competition elsewhere, and never yield this territory—it represents your best opportunity for victory.

Lesson 59
COERCE ANOTHER, DEFEAT YOURSELF

"We may simply fancy, like the blind horse moving in a circle round a mill, that we are making progress."

~ "Passive Resistance," *Hind Swaraj*, 1909

Question: Why did Gandhi disavow brute force as a means of achieving change?
Answer: Because brute force fails to achieve real and positive change.
Speculation: If brute force were capable of achieving real and positive change, Gandhi would have used it—because his objective was to create change.
Reality: But brute force doesn't work, so he didn't use it.

When Jesus told Peter that he who lives by the sword shall die by the sword, he was not making a moral plea so much as asserting a basic management principle—the same one Gandhi would articulate some two thousand years later: When we use brute force "it means that we want our opponent to do by force that which we desire but he does not. And if such a use of force is justifiable, surely he is entitled to do likewise by us. And so we should never come to an agreement. We may simply fancy, like the blind horse moving in a circle round a mill, that we are making progress."

As Gandhi pictured it, coercion by violence is the very definition of self-defeat because it hands your opponent the very weapon with which he may destroy you. The exercise of decisive, coercive action gives the impression of progress, but it is really self-defeating. That is why the effective CEO devises means of persuasion that demonstrate a benefit to all, including all those who take different sides in a dispute.

This win-win scenario can be either virtually impossible to achieve or so easy as to be self-evident:

- If the leader approaches the dispute on the terms dictated by the disputants—that is, *I want something, you want something else*—the win-win resolution is impossible.

- If, however, she approaches it on the terms dictated by the common good—the enterprise in which both disputants have a stake—then the resolution is self-evident.

The course that delivers genuine benefit to the enterprise is a winning course for all who have a stake in the enterprise. Any other resolution is incomplete and therefore a failure. Insofar as failure is damaging to the common good, accepting an incomplete resolution (regardless of the apparent benefit it may confer on one side versus the other) is self-defeating. Win-win is not just a desirable outcome; it is the only viable alternative to a failed outcome.

Lesson 60
KEEP YOUR PROMISES

> "Our pledge of non-violence excludes the possibility of future retaliation. Some of us seem, unfortunately, to have merely postponed the date of revenge."
>
> ~ "Non-violence," *Young India*, March 9, 1922

Change is the river in which we all swim. In business, the power of a contract or any other promise is as a hedge against change. A pledge of performance, of payment, of reward represents a still place in the ceaselessly roiling stream. Without a basis for confidence in the future of a promise there can be no confidence in the future, period. We would drift, subject to time, change, whim, opportunism, and the forces of greed and fear.

Gandhi saw his role not only as the instigator and inspirer of change, but also as the steward of stability. A leader's job is to manage change without bringing chaos down upon the enterprise. A big part of a CEO's job is to serve as the keeper of the promises, ensuring that they are not allowed to expire at will, in panic, or at the first whiff of fast money. If a pledge cannot be relied upon to govern the future, it is worthless. The future is the essence of any contract, agreement, or promise.

Gandhi understood that as difficult as it was to persuade his followers to adhere to their strenuous promise of nonviolence on their road to independence, it would be even harder for them to refrain from releasing a pent-up desire for revenge once the goal of independence had been achieved. It is one thing to promise not to use force when one has no force to use, but quite another to honor that promise once the power is in one's possession. Yet this is precisely when it is most important to keep to the pledge. It is not a mere matter of honor and ethics—though it is certainly that—but of averting a state of chaos that would paralyze all meaningful interaction. In the sphere of commerce, a business that makes pledges but fails to honor them through time is bound to fail. Chaos is never favorable to business.

■

Lesson 61
WIN THROUGH SURRENDER

> "My creed is non-violence under all circumstances. . . . it is self-suffering, not the suffering of the tyrant."
>
> ~ "Independence vs. Swaraj," *Young India,* January 12, 1928

"Generations to come will scarce believe that such a one as this ever in flesh and blood walked upon this earth," Albert Einstein wrote of Mohandas Gandhi. The notion that one would embrace self-suffering rather than inflict suffering on another, no matter how oppressive that other was, is reason enough for Einstein's wonder. However, even more astounding was the expectation—the fulfilled expectation—that self-suffering would ever defeat tyranny.

Gandhi's method of creating social change was as simple in concept as it was difficult in execution. Self-suffering deprives the oppressor of all power. You cannot stop a tyrant from hurting you, but if you are willing to endure the punishment and pain of non-compliance with tyranny, you defeat the tyrant by rendering his tools powerless.

A CEO rarely finds himself in a position in which he must endure physical self-suffering, yet this concept still has a vital lesson to teach all leaders: In dealing with any crisis, or in negotiating with even the most difficult person, begin by determining what you can control and what lies outside of your control. Then, focus only on what you can control. For example, if a vendor refuses to accommodate the constraints of your budget, waste no time in protracted negotiation; instead, identify another vendor or devise alternatives to acquiring what the vendor sells.

This seems obvious enough, and yet many CEOs and managers see such simple maneuvers, based on confining your actions to what you control, as acts of surrender. They cannot stand to lose a negotiation, and for them the negotiation becomes more important than the outcome it produces. This attitude, though self-defeating, is understandable. After all, most business leaders are naturally competitive. They define success in terms of winning or losing—and there is nothing inherently wrong with this if you don't define winning or losing in terms of the way you *feel*. Winning is not about the gratification of the ego—"bragging rights"—but about doing the best you can for your organization. Defined this way, winning may well entail "surrendering" in the case of one vendor and going on to another. Or it may consist of simply learning to live without the vendor's merchandise.

Struggling against forces, facts, and people beyond your influence presents no chance of altering reality in your favor. On the other hand, identifying what you can influence and then acting to influence it *does* impact reality, and if you manage the areas of your influence wisely, the changes you make will benefit you and your enterprise.

Lesson 62
REPLACE UNRELENTING COERCION WITH UNRELENTING TRUTH

"Our non-violence must not breed violence, hatred and ill-will."
~ "Non-violence," *Young India*, March 9, 1922

In his iconic novel of totalitarian dystopia, *1984*, George Orwell portrayed the ultimate power of the state this way: to compel an individual not merely to utter $2 + 2 = 5$ but actually to believe $2 + 2 = 5$. The problem with exercising this degree of power is that it must be wielded continuously, always backed by force and the threat of force. Maintaining belief in the manifestly false proposition $2 + 2 = 5$ requires unrelenting coercion.

Gandhi understood violence as the means of maintaining untruth among a people. If, by contrast, you intended to inculcate truth among this same group, Gandhi held that it had to be accomplished through the complete absence of violence or coercion of any kind. Introduce violence, and you introduce wrong—untruth—which will require continued and sustained violence to maintain.

When Gandhi asked independence-seeking Indians to welcome their opponents "to our political platforms as honoured guests," he was not appealing for civility merely for its own sake or because good manners are more comfortable than bad. His deeper belief was that only in an atmosphere free of violence, hatred, and ill-will would the revolutionary ideas he advocated be accepted freely as the truth. Once accepted in this manner, the ideas would not, in turn, breed violence, hatred, and ill-will. Absent these negatives, no coercion would be required to maintain the desired change in society. It would simply be accepted as the truth: $2 + 2 = 4$.

With each coercive act, a CEO, manager, or supervisor erodes his real power and instead multiplies the ongoing difficulties of his job. The most effective leaders devise means of creating a climate of compliance in which everyone is treated with respect and in which all opinions are welcomed. Disagreements are not allowed to become disagreeable. Issues, not personalities, are made the focus of discussion and debate. Everyone is given a voice. This does not mean that all decisions must embody every opinion, but it does mean that an authoritative ear and mind are given to every voice.

Restraint is the surest mark of true leadership power. Compliance won is always more effective—and far easier to sustain—than compliance coerced.

■

Principles and Pragmatism

Gandhi's life was an epic experiment in principled living. Whereas most sincere, thinking people contemplate adherence to principle, only to conclude that the "realities" of modern life make living strictly according to principle impossible or, at least, impractical, Gandhi went ahead and tried. That he succeeded to such an impressive degree is in part a testament to the strength of his determined will and in part the result of his clear conception of a set of worthwhile principles; but Gandhi also succeeded because he managed the application of principle with a pragmatic eye toward the dynamic, fluid nature of the day to day. He continually tested his principles against the objectives and goals he had formulated for his enterprise. Depending on the outcome, he strengthened, modified, and even rejected certain principles as he devised new ones. That was one level of strategy and tactics. It rested, however, on a bedrock of ideals on which there could be neither alteration nor compromise.

This chapter highlights one remarkable leader's efforts to formulate and implement productive, valuable principles. In this study in judgment, a set of examples illustrates the art of balancing principles and pragmatism to produce meaningful and productive change.

■

Lesson 63
THINK UTOPIAN

> "If Euclid's point, though incapable of being drawn by human agency, has an imperishable value, my picture has its own for mankind to live. Let India live for this true picture, though never realizable in its completeness."
>
> ~ "Independence," *Harijan,* July 28, 1946

"Utopia," as we learn in school, is a pun derived from two Greek words—homonyms, one meaning "good place," the other "no place" or "nowhere." The gist of the pun is that utopia is an entirely imaginary ideal, a good place that exists nowhere. For this reason, idealistic visions of a wonderful but nonexistent reality are often mocked as "utopian" and dismissed out of hand.

Gandhi, whose life's work, winning Indian independence, made actual what had seemed to many a wild fantasy, never abandoned utopian thinking—even after independence had become a fact. He cheerfully confessed that the complete picture of the world as he imagined it was, like Euclid's geometric point, "never realizable." Yet he asserted that, as with Euclid's ideal, his utopian vision was valuable and not to be rejected just because it could never be completed in the material world.

"We must have a proper picture of what we want," he wrote, "before we can have something approaching it." Utopian thought is not to be scorned just because it can never be fully realized. That the ideal can be *approached*, even if never attained, is of great value in itself. You should not hesitate to set the bar impossibly high, but you must not brand as failures achievements that fall short of this impossible height. Provided that you dream ambitiously enough, the approach—not the attainment—defines success.

■

Lesson 64
FORMULATE A HIERARCHY OF OPTIONS

"I do believe that where there is only a choice between cowardice and violence I would advise violence."

~ "The Doctrine of the Sword," *Young India*, August 4, 1920

Few men are more powerfully principled than Mohandas Gandhi, yet even he refused to relinquish his free will to choices rigidly dictated by principle. He thought through and formulated a hierarchy of options that depended on particular circumstances at a particular time. History's most famous apostle of nonviolence, Gandhi nevertheless recognized a circumstance in which violence was the preferable option—namely, when the only other choice was cowardice. "Thus when my eldest son asked me what he should have done when I was almost fatally assaulted in 1908, whether he should have run away and seen me killed or whether he should have used his physical force which he could and wanted to use, and defended me, I told him that it was his duty to defend me even by using violence." Gandhi himself supported the British in the Second (Great) Boer War—serving as an army ambulance driver—the Zulu Uprising, and World War I, and he proclaimed his advocacy of "training in arms for those who believe in the method of violence" because he would "rather have India resort to arms in order to defend her honour than that she should in a cowardly manner become or remain a helpless witness to her own dishonor." Without question, Gandhi believed "that nonviolence is infinitely superior to violence," and he cautioned against mistaking "physical capacity" for a source of true strength, which (he wrote) "comes from an indomitable will," not an abundance of muscle or a stock of weaponry. Yet despite his loathing for violent methods, he could not rule them out in absolutely every circumstance.

That as passionate an advocate of principle as Gandhi drew the line at relinquishing judgment to principle—that he allowed the possibility of choosing violence in some specific circumstances—is a powerful lesson for any principled leader. Rigidity in any form is dangerous and destructive. Worthwhile and clearly articulated principles should guide all decisions, but they should never be permitted to force a decision, since a forced decision is no decision at all. Leadership requires the exercise of judgment. To surrender judgment to principle, policy, or ideology is to surrender leadership itself.

■

Lesson 65
REJECT THE FETISH OF IDEOLOGY

"Even [a] good thing can be ridden to death if it is made a fetish."
~ "The Law of Swadeshi," *Young India,* June 18, 1931

Swadeshi, Gandhi's doctrine of self-sufficiency, was aimed primarily at achieving economic independence from Britain and other foreign powers. A tireless promoter of swadeshi, Gandhi nevertheless cautioned against transforming it into a "fetish" by rejecting "foreign manufactures merely because they are foreign" or "to go on wasting national time and money to promote manufactures in one's country for which it is not suited." The first step toward swadeshi was to identify those goods that could be economically and effectively manufactured domestically and also to identify those imported goods that the people could do without. Both were steps toward economic independence. Yet Gandhi also recognized that some foreign goods would remain useful and economical, or simply beyond the capacity of India itself to produce. In these cases, stubborn adherence to swadeshi worked against the national welfare.

Principle is important to any organization, but it is neither profitable nor ethical to sacrifice people to principle. Adherence to ideology must end where individual welfare and the collective welfare of the enterprise begin. Service and stewardship are the cardinal duties of a CEO or other manager. Formulation of ideology and adherence to principles are important aids and adjuncts to the effective discharge of this duty, but neither ideology nor principle is an end in itself. The declaration one often hears from the stubborn and high minded—"It's not the such-and-such, but the principle of the thing"—may well betray a leader who has made a fetish of ideology by allowing principle to come before the good of the organization and of the individuals within the organization.

Serve people, not ideas. This is the one item of ideology that is of unfailing value to all, at all times.

■

Lesson 66
NEVER LET *BEST* STAND IN THE WAY OF *GOOD*

> "You are impatient. I cannot afford to be likewise."
>
> ~ "The Congress and Its Officials," *Hind Swaraj*, 1909

In his quest for Indian home rule and independence, Gandhi welcomed the support of all who could be helpful, including Indian advocates of independence and members of the British administration who were willing to yield some degree of home rule, no matter how incomplete. This attitude led many to protest Gandhi's apparent willingness to compromise—to accept crumbs when the object was the entire loaf. To such protesters, Gandhi responded. "You are impatient. I cannot afford to be likewise." He cited an old proverb that taught "the tree does not grow in one day." He explained that for anyone who disdains to "hear about the well-wishers of India"—including those well-wishers whose sentiments did not extend to full independence—"Home Rule is yet far away. If we had many like you, we would never make any advance."

It is praiseworthy to demand great things. It is laudable to harbor big ambitions and bold dreams. But it is destructive and self-defeating to expect instant fulfillment of all that you want, especially if this prompts you to reject progress—however incremental and limited—toward complete realization of your goal. For Gandhi, patience did not mean suspending ambitions and aspirations; rather, it meant enduring compromises and half-steps as long as these were at least inclined toward the ultimate goal. To be patient was nothing more or less than to recognize the necessary dimension of time in every plan. Accepting a crumb now does not require forever renouncing the whole loaf. In time, crumb by crumb, everything can be yours. If your destination is a mile away, you would be foolish to refuse to take the first step just because that single step did not span the entire mile.

Make demands, but measure them through time. In some situations, time is of the essence, and it is almost always necessary to weigh patience against urgency. However, there is never a valid reason to reject what is good because it is not best. Instead, plan your course so that you may move from one good to another on your way to the best.

Improvement—a high-value management goal—is a function of effort made through time. Rejecting improvement because it moves from good to better instead of instantly leaping from good to best is likely to produce total paralysis. In such a static state, "progress," "development," and "evolution" are mere words, labels for impossible ideals. To reject the good in quest of the best denies you both better and best.

Lesson 67
THERE IS NO VIRTUE IN NECESSITY

"The mouse is not non-violent towards the cat."
~ "Problems of Non-Violence," *Navajivan*, August 9, 1925

The inability—lack of capacity, want of means—to commit an unethical act does not constitute ethical behavior. "The mouse is not non-violent towards the cat," Gandhi wrote. "At heart, he always has a feeling of violence towards the cat. He cannot kill the latter because he is weak." The inability of the mouse to kill the cat is not a virtue. In the relationship between cat and mouse, only the cat—who has the strength to kill the mouse—can practice true nonviolence by refraining from doing harm to the rodent. Only the cat can claim virtue in the absence of violence.

As a leader, you need to develop a keen eye for necessity and act accordingly. But acting in accordance with necessity confers no special virtue, even if what is necessary happens to harmonize with a set of cherished and laudable principles. It is important to remain mindful of the distinction between necessity and virtue so that you can more accurately evaluate each decision you make. It is even more important, however, never to avoid a necessary action simply because it falls short of the ideal.

■

Lesson 68
PROCESS DEFINES RESULT

"Will you still say that means do not matter?"
~ "Brute Force," *Hind Swaraj*, 1909

Throughout his long campaign for nonviolent revolution in India, Gandhi repeatedly confronted the argument that any and all means may be used to attain a laudable goal. In his chapter on "Brute Force" in *Hind Swaraj*, his seminal treatise on Indian home rule, Gandhi phrased the question this way: "Why should we not obtain our goal, which is good, by any means whatsoever, even by using violence?"

Instead of answering this question with a statement of the abstract moral principle that means are inseparable from ends, Gandhi proposed three possible means by which he might take your pocket watch from you:

> If I want to deprive you of your watch, I shall certainly have to fight you for it; if I want to buy your watch, I shall have to pay you for it; and if I want a gift I shall have to plead for it; and, according to the means I employ, the watch is stolen property, my own property, or a donation. Thus we see three different results from three different means.

All of these results achieve the same physical end—the transfer of the watch from you to me—but, Gandhi asked, "Will you still say that means do not matter?"

Means adhere to ends. The process defines the results of the process. You cannot produce wholesome bread if you knead the dough with filthy hands. The CEO who abuses those she is charged to lead may move the company to certain specific accomplishments, but a dirty process diminishes the practitioner and thus erodes the sustainability of the enterprise.

■

Lesson 69

INSTRUMENTS ARE NOT VALUES

"It is merely an instrument, and an instrument may be well used
or abused."

~ "Education," *Hind Swaraj*, 1909

Many students of the campaign for Indian independence were disturbed that Gandhi made no special effort to promote education as
part of a program of social reform. After all, it seemed self-evident
that education was an absolute good and, without question, a desirable value. Gandhi responded, "It is merely an instrument, and an
instrument may be well used or abused." He explained that just as
the "same instrument that may be used to cure a patient may be used
to take his life," so education, misused, can bring harm. "To give millions [in India] a knowledge of English is to enslave them. . . . Is it not
a sad commentary that we should have to speak of Home Rule in a
foreign tongue?"

Wise leadership requires both the ability and the willingness to
distinguish values from instruments. The first are desirable goals
and guides; the second are morally neutral means of achieving or
avoiding, explaining or distorting such values. Consider one of the
most common and most commonly reviled institutions of the corporate workplace: the meeting. If you ever want to see a collection
of eyes roll in unison, walk into a room full of business people and
ask them to tell you about the last meeting they attended. After
you've witnessed enough orbiting pupils, just say two words—"productive meeting"—and you will get a brand new reaction: mocking
laughter, bordering on the hysterical.

Not only do all too many business meetings waste time and
effort, people go into them actually *expecting* to waste time and effort.
The business meeting is a classic example of the self-fulfilling
prophecy. The reason? Meetings are widely regarded as an expression of certain desirable values—teamwork, brainstorming, giving

everyone a stake in the enterprise, and so on—rather than what they truly are: instruments for achieving particular goals. If you want to rehabilitate the classic business meeting, begin treating it as an instrument, as a means rather than an end, and two things are likely to happen: First, your organization will convene fewer meetings; second, those that do take place will be *useful and productive*.

Once you untangle values from instruments, you will no longer take your management assumptions for granted. Rather, this will enable you to approach them more critically, and you will almost certainly gain a clearer understanding of the values worth holding and developing as well as the tools best suited to advancing those values. Furthermore, you will discover that you have gained a more rational and truthful approach to managing the indispensable resources of any endeavor: time, money, and people.

■

Lesson 70
ETHICS IS THE OIL OF ENTERPRISE

"We who seek justice will have to do justice to others."
~ "The Congress and Its Officials," *Hind Swaraj*, 1909

Ethics is as essential to the sustained operation of a business as oil is to the sustained operation of a machine. Neither can be thought of as a mere adjunct. In business, ethics is no more subordinate to profit than oil is subordinate to gasoline as a requisite to the operation of a motor. Without both oil and gas, the engine stops; without both profit and ethics, the business seizes up.

The difference between profit and ethics is that profit may be the result of any number of pragmatic decisions, different in differing situations, whereas ethics is not subject to pragmatic decisions but rather founded on the permanent, universal principle of justice. An ethical enterprise treats everyone—employees, customers, shareholders, vendors, even competitors—justly, in all circumstances. The failure of one product line to turn a profit one quarter is not likely to make a business forever unprofitable, but treating one of your stakeholders unjustly will have a lasting effect on the company's reputation. Profit and loss are balanced against one another. If the profit side of the ledger is greater than the loss side, the company is profitable. Justice and injustice cannot be calculated this way. A single unethical act, if allowed to stand uncorrected, unbalances and outweighs everything else.

Gandhi taught that ethical conduct is a continuum along which it is impossible to divide means from ends. Considered in the context of ethics, means and ends are, in fact, one and the same. An enterprise that proposes to present itself as ethical must deliver ethics in everything it does. An enterprise that expects to receive ethical treatment—from employees, customers, shareholders, vendors, and even competitors—must treat all of these constituents ethically.

While ethics, like justice, is perfect in concept, it is not always possible to deliver it flawlessly. This fact can never be allowed to excuse deliberately unethical conduct. Consider: A product warranty does not guarantee a perfect piece of merchandise, but it does guarantee replacement or repair of any imperfect item. Likewise, an ethical business cannot guarantee that every transaction every time will be perfectly just, but it must guarantee that it will endeavor in good faith to correct any injustice—every time and in every case. An ethical firm never walks away from an unethical result. There is far too much value at stake.

■

Lesson 71

ASK AND ANSWER THE QUESTION OF COMMITMENT

"He perhaps puts an emphasis on the result, whereas I put [it] on
the means."

~ "Interview to an Egyptian," January 22, 1937

In the long aftermath of Russia's 1917 Bolshevik Revolution, Gandhi was frequently asked about his views on communism. His invariable reply was that its embrace of violence repelled him. In 1937, however, he conceded that he did believe in "non-violent communism," explaining that if it "came without any violence, it would be welcome" because "no property would be held by anybody except on behalf of the people and for the people."

Following up on this response, the interviewer asked Gandhi if there was any "difference of opinion" between him and his chief apostle Jawaharlal Nehru (destined to become the first prime minister of independent India). Gandhi's answer is extraordinarily revealing. He explained that there was "a difference in emphasis. He perhaps puts an emphasis on the result, whereas I put [it] on the means." Gandhi allowed that Nehru probably believed he, Gandhi, was "putting over-emphasis on non-violence, whereas [Nehru], though he believes in non-violence, would want to have socialism by other means if it was impossible to have it by non-violence." Gandhi could not accept this alternative. He insisted that his own "emphasis on non-violence" was "one of principle" and that even if he were "assured that we could have independence by violence," he would "refuse to have it. It won't be real independence."

The question raised here is whether adherence to a principle must be absolute or whether it can be a matter of degree. Gandhi's position was that principle demanded the greatest possible commitment (though even he confessed that principle must sometimes yield to urgent need and common sense), whereas Nehru (as Gandhi saw it) believed a principle could survive even with conditional commitment. Gandhi believed that to compromise a principle was to compromise the means to an end, and to the degree that means was compromised, the end would be devalued, even to the point of becoming a counterfeit. Independence achieved by violent means would not be genuine independence, but rather a ratification of violence. As such, instead of being truly independent, the people will have made themselves slaves to violence. In contrast to this position, Nehru held that to achieve a very good end, a compromise of means could be justified if no better choice were possible.

For Gandhi, the issue was really quite simple. Even the noblest, most desirable of ends does not justify a destructive compromise of means. While this position must evoke admiration from all, most of us identify more closely with Nehru's position, which seems more compatible with what we would call the "real world." Both Gandhi and Nehru were good and well-intentioned leaders, and the questions their difference in this matter raises must occupy any leader, manager, or CEO who comes after them. They are questions not merely worth pondering, but questions that demand deliberate and supremely self-aware answers.

Lesson 72
DEMOLISH THE DEVIATION, NOT THE ORIGINAL

"In order to demolish this distortion let us not seek to demolish the original."

~Speech at Tanjore, September 16, 1927

In explaining to his audience at Tanjore, India, the meaning of *varnashrama*—which he described as a traditional Hindu foundation for the belief in the inherent equality of all humankind—Gandhi acknowledged that as the concept was "at present understood and practiced," it was nothing more than "a monstrous parody of the original." He cautioned, however, that in seeking to demolish the deviation from the original there was the danger of demolishing the original itself. This had to be avoided at all costs.

Organizations lose many good ideas and many good programs when CEOs overreact to a deviation from a plan, model, or prototype. Instead of responding with a course correction or a product modification, there is a great danger of yielding to the temptation to scrap everything and start from scratch—or simply abandon the program or idea altogether.

When something goes wrong and diverges from the expected, neither panic nor even a well-founded sense of urgency should be allowed to prompt reflexive overreaction. Instead, use a measured approach:

• Begin by assessing the deviation. Does it really indicate that the underlying idea is unworkable? Or is it the result of drifting unacceptably from a good idea?

• If you determine that the underlying idea is worth saving, work backward from the current problem until you have found where the policy, program, or product has strayed from the original idea.

• Confine your efforts at correction to everything after the deviation, thereby preserving as much of the original as possible.

It is always a serious mistake to turn a blind eye to a problem, including deviation from anticipated or desired results. It is also a grave error to deny the possibility that a bad outcome is the result of a bad idea. However, it is worse to throw away the value and creative labor that went into an idea because of results produced by the flawed implementation of that idea. And, certainly, worst of all is to deliberately discard a potential opportunity based solely on present inadequacies.

Paradoxically, true innovation requires a certain strong conservatism that is manifested as an extreme reluctance ever to abandon effort or abort creativity. In fact, the process of innovation actually calls for greater patience and more endurance than that required to maintain the status quo.

■

Lesson 73
EVEN AN IDEALIST MUST SOMETIMES CHOOSE PRAGMATISM

"Where there is danger from tigers, wolves and so on, then killing them becomes inevitable."

~ "Problems of Non-Violence," *Navajivan*, August 9, 1925

Sincere people peppered Gandhi with questions as to "which acts may be termed violent and which non-violent, and what is one's duty at a particular time." Gandhi did his best to answer these, and he was particularly intrigued by a question from someone he described as a "Punjabi gentleman." The man had asked him what "should be done when tigers, wolves and other wild beasts come and carry away other animals or human beings? Or, what should be done about germs in water?" Gandhi replied that in the face of danger from animals or germs, both have to be destroyed. This, he admitted, was not a happy solution, but an inevitable one. Even so, "Violence which is inevitable does not therefore cease to be so and become non-violence. It has to be recognized as violence." Gandhi expressed his belief that "it would be best if we could contrive to survive without destroying tigers, wolves, etc. However, who could do so?"

At some point, principle must yield to common sense, and the possible must be allowed to trump the impossible. It is up to the leader of the enterprise to recognize when this point has been reached. Having reached it, however, and having acted on common sense or on the basis of possibility or feasibility (versus impossibility or impracticality), you must still recognize that you are acting on necessity, not principle.

Gandhi said that even necessary violence is still violence, and we should keep looking for ways to narrow the scope of violence whenever possible. Similarly, when an expedient choice becomes the necessary choice—the only feasible or even possible choice—it behooves a leader to search for a more desirable, "principled" alternative to be implemented in the future. Common sense should be regarded as the lowest common denominator, not the height of performance. It is at best an acceptable minimum standard, which may indeed be a very long way from what is desirable, let alone optimal.

■

Reject Tyranny, Take Responsibility

Most business professionals appreciate the power and the importance of branding, whether the brand in question is a product, a service—or yourself. A brand is a label on the outside that announces to the world the presence of something good, valuable, and desirable on the inside. A brand is a positive identity. If you fail to acquire such an identity, others will invariably apply an identity to you. That is the message of the first lesson in this chapter, and it is also the crux of the critical truth Gandhi discovered about the relationship of the individual to the powers that be. You either label yourself—define your own identity—or the state will label you. In Gandhi's India, that label was *victim*, so he offered his people a stern alternative: Tear off the label. Choose not to be a victim. Turn your back on the government, its institutions, its merchandise, and its laws.

Improbable as it may seem, the experience of Gandhi in India is a masterful example of marketing and branding—albeit on an epic scale and for the highest of stakes. The lessons drawn from that experience are especially valuable to the CEO or manager, whose product is not only himself but the organization he leads. Both are in urgent need of the right label, the right brand.

■

Lesson 74
CREATE GENUINE RELATIONSHIPS, NOT FALSE LABELS

"The bond of the slave is snapped the moment he considers himself to be a free being."

~Speech at AICC (All-India Congress Committee) meeting,

August 8, 1942

At the heart of Gandhi's campaign for the liberation of India was the mission of raising the consciousness of the Indian people above the persuasive power of the British colonial government. That government labeled Indians subjects of the British Crown. To the extent that an Indian accepted this label as the truth, it did accurately describe his relation to the Crown. However, the moment he no longer accepted the label, the label ceased to be true. Despite what the British authorities asserted and even believed, that person was no longer a subject of the Crown, the label thereby rendered meaningless.

Slavery, Gandhi realized, requires both an enslaver and a slave. In other words, slavery requires a person willing to designate another person as a slave as well as another person who is willing to be so designated. Remove either partner in this relationship, and slavery ceases to exist. "The bond of the slave is snapped the moment he considers himself to be a free being," Gandhi told his AICC audience in 1942. "He will plainly tell the master: 'I was your bondslave till this moment, but I am a slave no longer.'" The self-liberated slave may even acknowledge that the would-be master "may kill me if you like," but if he does, he will be a master without a slave—and therefore no master at all.

The truth of a relationship does not inhere in the label one person attaches to another, but in the mutual acceptance of the label by the parties in the relationship. Loyalty and collaboration can never be imposed or presumed—they are qualities of a relationship between or among people, and, by definition, all parties involved must accept the validity of the relationship and hold the same conception of it. Whereas creating a valid relationship requires the universal consent and understanding of all involved, ending that same relationship calls only for the withdrawal of one of the parties. The old labels may cling—including *boss* and *employee*—but they no longer accurately describe the relationship, no more than the tomato-soup label accurately describes the contents of an empty can.

■

Lesson 75
DECLINE TO BE A VICTIM

"The English have not taken India; we have given it to them."
~ "What Is Swaraj?" *Hind Swaraj*, 1909

Gandhi understood injustice, not as a crime inflicted by one person (or people) against another, but as a transaction between two parties. The English, he wrote, "are not in India because of their strength but because we keep them." For Indians to blame them as conquerors would be to renounce India's responsibility for its own victimization. For without a victim, there can be no victimizer. "If I am in the habit of drinking *bhang* [an intoxicant derived from cannabis] and a seller thereof sells it to me, am I to blame him or myself?" More important, "By blaming the seller, shall I be able to avoid the habit?"

The first fatal step toward becoming a victim is to relinquish responsibility for your own welfare. As Gandhi saw it, the victimizer's strength is a gift unwittingly presented to him by the victim.

Among the CEO's most important responsibilities is to avoid the complacency that thoughtlessly yields power to others. Instead of blaming others for harm done, it makes much more sense to exercise vigilance and avoid entering a transaction that puts you in the role of victim. Let no one define you, your values, or your goals. Retain the initiative in these things, and you will enter into each transaction as an equal. Relinquish the initiative, and you allow yourself to be cast in the victim's role.

But who would willingly yield something so important as the initiative in which one's identity resides?

Gandhi believed that India kept the English "for our base self-interest. We like their commerce." India, he argued, had long exchanged freedom for trade. Because it had received what it bargained for—namely, trade with the English—India did not always count itself a victim, even though the bargain was a lopsided one. In much the same way, many CEOs steer their enterprises into bad bargains, thus making their organization a victim because they see only one side of the bargain. They see the object they want but underestimate its actual cost. The result is a victimization in which the victim fails to realize that he is a victim. In such a transaction, who is more to blame: the victim or the victimizer?

■

Lesson 76
TAKE RESPONSIBILITY, THEN TAKE COMMAND

"But I make a mistake. How can Manchester be blamed?"

~ "Machinery," *Hind Swaraj*, 1909

What Gandhi described as India's slavery to Britain was not just political, but also economic. Britain had made Indians dependent on British trade and British exports. "It is machinery that has impoverished India," Gandhi wrote. "It is difficult to measure the harm that Manchester [center of the British export textile industry] has done to us. It is due to Manchester that Indian handicraft has all but disappeared."

Export goods made India less self-reliant. However, Gandhi did not stop with this point. "But I make a mistake," he continued. "How can Manchester be blamed? We wore Manchester cloth and this is why Manchester wove it." On behalf of India, Gandhi took responsibility for the impoverishment he initially blamed on the Manchester exports. While it is true that Manchester enabled the loss of Indian handicraft, it was Indian demand for Manchester goods—Indian complicity in the export economy—that completed the destructive transaction.

There is more than an ethical benefit in taking responsibility. The people of India were powerless to prevent Manchester from milling textiles, but they could refuse to buy such imports and weave homespun cloth instead. By taking responsibility for its part of the transaction, India was empowered to act productively. Gandhi began a movement to reawaken traditional Indian weaving—not for sale but for home use. If every household wove its own cloth, there would be no need for Manchester imports. This would be a major, wholly nonviolent disengagement from—and liberation from—British economic domination.

Blame achieves nothing, whereas taking responsibility lets you take command by identifying those aspects of a transaction, a project, or a problem that are under your control or on which you can act. Assigning blame is almost always valueless, whereas taking responsibility offers great value insofar as it empowers you to act productively.

■

Lesson 77
BE POWER'S STEWARD, NOT ITS SLAVE

> "We are opposing the intoxication of power, that is, the blind application of law, and not authority as such. The difference must never be lost sight of."
>
> ~ "Instructions to Volunteers," Satyagraha Camp, Nadiad,
>
> April 17, 1918

Oppose power? You might just as well attempt to oppose gravity. For what gravity is in nature, power is in human affairs: a force and a fact. All governance, whether of a nation or of a company, is about the control, management, manipulation, and apportionment of power. Power is the given—the questions are who will control it and how they will control it.

Gandhi was anything but a fool, and he was certainly never foolish enough to protest power. To have tried to do so would have been futile, and he knew it. Instead, he led opposition to the "intoxication of power . . . the blind application of law, and not authority as such." Never be ashamed of the authority of leadership, but always remember your duty to steward that authority. Use it arbitrarily, blindly, or for its own sake, and you invite opposition. Use it with thoughtful restraint and with specific application, and you invite compliance and cooperation. It is the mismanagement of power, not power itself, that creates resistance and draws opposition.

■

Lesson 78
EXPLOIT THE POWER OF DISSATISFACTION

"This discontent is a very useful thing."
~ "Discontent and Unrest," *Hind Swaraj*, 1909

You would be hard pressed to find a management guru who promotes discontent. "Customer satisfaction"–whether the "customer" is external (a consumer, a client) or internal (a colleague, a boss)–is an article of faith for virtually every business.

And it *should* be an article of faith for virtually every business. Your customers evaluate each transaction with you as an exchange of value for value, a commodity largely measured in perceived satisfaction. This principle, however, should not prompt you to neglect the power of customer *dissatisfaction*. "As long as a man is contented with his present lot," Gandhi recognized, "so long is it difficult to persuade him to come out of it." In other words, it's not easy to sell something new to a happy man. "Therefore it is that every reform must be preceded by discontent. We throw away the things we have only when we cease to like them."

Innovation is driven by discontent. Had our ancestors been content to drag heavy loads, the wheel would have been a very hard sell. Make it your business to identify discontent among all your customers, external and internal, and among your potential customers–the segment of the market you have yet to penetrate. Having found it, explore it, embrace it, and work with it. Let discontent drive the innovation of your enterprise.

Monitor the state of satisfaction *and* the state of dissatisfaction among all of your stakeholders. Don't defend or try to justify the causes of discontent. Welcome this negative response as an opportunity to improve, to convert dissatisfaction into satisfaction. Customers are grateful for receiving consistent satisfaction, but they are even more enthusiastic when they perceive significant improvement. If the performance baseline is already high, congratulations. But you will have even more cause for celebration if you manage to raise below-par performance to the level of excellence. All of your customers will recognize, talk about, and act upon such a leap.

■

11

Revaluation as Revolution

The American Revolution spanned eight years, from 1775 to 1783—by any measure a long war, a shooting war, violent and destructive. Yet, in 1818, John Adams wrote, "Revolution was effected before the war commenced." He explained further. "The Revolution was in the minds and hearts of the people . . . This radical change in the principles, opinions, sentiments, and affections of the people was the real American Revolution."

Adams would have struck a sympathetic chord with Gandhi, who believed that revolution lies in the revaluation of the reality that surrounds us. Revolution begins with questioning that reality and deciding whether or not to "cooperate" with it. On the part of the makers of the revolution, there need be no violence. Yet Gandhi knew that even revolution as revaluation would not come easily or cheaply. He knew there would be shooting and beating and other violence, all meted out against the revolutionaries, who would not retaliate but only persist in noncooperation. The bloodshed was a *consequence* of the revolution, not the *substance* of the revolution, which took place entirely in the minds and hearts of the people.

CEOs, managers, and other business leaders put themselves at the head of a continual reappraisal of values, goals, strategy, and tactics. Insofar as they endeavor to lead change, they incite and direct the revolution. Here are lessons in how it begins and how it is won.

■

Lesson 79
BRING YOUR ENTERPRISE OUT OF ITS SHELL

"Castes are numerous. They are man-made. They undergo constant change."

~ "Caste and Varna," November 28, 1935

In Gandhi's time, all defenders of India's caste system sooner or later fell back on religion, asserting that the social stratification of caste was created not by men, but by God; therefore, the faithful had no choice but to adhere to it. Gandhi sought to refute this position by pointing out that castes were by no means changeless, absolute, or eternal but, on the contrary, were themselves the products of change and were therefore obviously "man-made." Like anything artificial, castes could be discarded when they were determined to be either useless or harmful.

Like many beliefs that some hold sacred and absolute, caste was really an empty shell. When a hermit crab outgrows the shell he occupies, it is time for him to leave it behind, empty. Outworn ideas are to be shed and left behind, freeing the organization to find a new form. As we saw in Lesson 37 (Chapter 5), Gandhi recommended replacing the empty shell of caste with the concept of the *varnas*, the traditional four-part Hindu division of society. He explained that, like the caste system, varnas served to structure society, but they did so without the harsh, irrational, and harmful restrictions that retard progress. Gandhi considered the varnas structures harmonious with nature itself and therefore a true alternative to the false, empty shell of caste.

[146]

Emulate Gandhi in questioning every value, policy, rule, and goal of your organization. Do so, not with an eye toward simply rejecting them, but of revitalizing or replacing them. If an old shell has been the only home your organization has known, it may be difficult to coax people out of it, regardless of how cramped and uncomfortable it may be. Demonstrate to them that the shell is neither eternal nor absolute. You cannot expect people to venture into a void—and why should they?—so the call to change must be more than a call to abandon the old and outworn. Make it a simultaneous call to embrace something new and better. Strangely, most people have to be cajoled into their own liberation, but in the end they are grateful for the change, and the enterprise much improved.

Lesson 80
TO SEE INSIDE, STEP OUTSIDE

> "[The civil resister] invites imprisonment and other uses of force against himself. This he does because and when he finds the bodily freedom he seemingly enjoys to be an intolerable burden. He argues to himself that a State allows personal freedom only in so far as the citizen submits to its regulations."
>
> ~ "The Momentous Issue," *Young India*, November 10, 1921

The state seems all powerful only to those who take for granted that they must obey the authority of the state. If the state is a box, those who live within it see only the confines of the box. Yet manage to get yourself outside of the box, and you instantly understand—as Gandhi did—that all the authority of the state comes from the people who accept its authority. "An out and out civil resister," Gandhi wrote, "simply ignores the authority of the State." The state, as he sees it, defines "freedom" as not being in prison, and it allows citizens to remain "free" in this sense as long as they obey the state's dictates. True freedom, however, is not to be found in unconditional obedience to authority. Therefore, prison—the state's punishment for disobedience—comes to seem a place of greater liberty than a life lived outside of prison walls but within the much closer confines of unquestioning obedience.

Innovation has less to do with visionary genius than it does with recognizing the relativity of your own particular point of view. If you believe that there is no possible alternative to the dictates of the state, that these dictates are therefore absolute, then the path of passive resistance will be meaningless to you. Dare to ask the question, "Is there an alternative to the dictates of the state?" and passive resistance will begin to make an abundance of good sense.

Gandhi's boldest efforts at bringing about sweeping social and political change began by questioning the absolute nature of certain realities and then asking what would happen if these realities were treated differently from what is expected or even required. He climbed outside of the box in order to look back inside.

Innovation begins by deliberately changing your perspective. Ask why Step A must be completed before Step B. If you can come up with no better answer than, "Because that's the way it has always been," then ask, "What if I put Step B before Step A?" The answer may be a vision of disaster, or it may lead to productive innovation. The only way to find out is, like Gandhi, to dare ask the questions few ever think of asking.

■

Lesson 81
ARGUE AGAINST YOURSELF

> "We rarely find people arguing against themselves."
>
> ~ "Civilization," *Hind Swaraj*, 1909

"Those who are intoxicated by modern civilization are not likely to write against it. Their care will be to find out facts and arguments in support of it. And this they do unconsciously, believing it to be true," Gandhi began his critique of modern civilization in *Hind Swaraj*.

His insight extends beyond his critique, however. We cannot help but defend what we believe and what we believe in. Intoxicated by our own vision, we hunt for facts and arguments in support of it as we exclude those that work against it. We are not consciously dishonest, but unconsciously biased. We see only what we want (or believe we need) to see.

As a CEO, manager, or other leader, your responsibility is to look beyond what your subjectivity comfortably tells you is true. The only reliable way to discharge this responsibility adequately is to do precisely what Gandhi says is rare: Argue against yourself. Before making any important decision, acquire the habit of arguing as thoroughly as possible the contrary of the course toward which you are inclined. Do not share your argument. Playing devil's advocate should be a game of solitaire. The reason for this stealth is that, when you are finally prepared to make your decision, you must present a seamlessly decisive front to the world. Before you reach this point, however, do your best to tear down your own most cherished assumptions. If they begin to come apart under your own assault, withhold your decision until you have examined all alternatives. If, however, your beliefs emerge intact, act on them with confidence.

■

Lesson 82

ANSWER NO QUESTION UNTIL YOU'VE MADE IT YOUR OWN

"You have put the question well, but the answer is not easy."

~ "The Congress and Its Officials," *Hind Swaraj*, 1909

We take for granted that every question demands an answer—and the quicker the better. As most of us see it, the desirable tempo of business is as fast as possible. Providing an immediate response to every question seems, on the face of it, a "best practice" in any enterprise.

The problem is that an answer is only as good as the question it answers, and you cannot always depend on getting good questions. You can work around this, however, if you make a question better by making it your own. Using this tactic, you do not merely provide an answer but enable understanding—both yours and the questioner's. You turn a demand-and-response into a genuinely useful instance of communication.

Learn from Gandhi, who never allowed himself to be pressured into an immediate response. For example, when asked about India's apparent eagerness for freedom from British imperial domination, Gandhi—although he passionately desired home rule as a step toward complete independence—did not yield to the temptation to answer with an obvious and simple "Yes, India wants home rule." Instead, he made the questioner's question his own by thoughtfully expanding and refining it, so that it could be answered with the degree of complexity and illumination it deserved. Gandhi explained the difficulty of gauging national opinion by citing the example of so-called newspaper reporting. He allowed that, "One of the objects of a newspaper is to understand popular feeling and to give expression to it," but then went on to enumerate the newspaper's two additional objects: "to arouse among the people certain desirable sentiments" and "fearlessly to expose popular defects." According to Gandhi, answering the apparently simple and direct question, "Does India want home rule?" required "the exercise of all . . . three functions." To answer the question, one must express the people's will as it exists, but, in addition, "certain sentiments will need to be fostered, and defects will have to be brought to light."

As was his way, Gandhi added enormous value to the original question, transforming it into the framework for the sophisticated and nuanced discussion its subject requires. For us, the moral of this exchange is crucial: Never let yourself be boxed in or your subject limited by a question posed to you. Don't evade the question or withhold an answer. Instead, remake, rework, and redefine the question so that you can give the fullest, most useful, and most accurate answer possible—an answer that delivers the greatest value to the questioner, to you, and to your enterprise.

■

Lesson 83
BUILD ON WHAT YOU HAVE

> "We believe that those who are discontented with the slowness of their parents and are angry because the parents would not run with their children are considered disrespectful to their parents."
>
> ~ "The Congress and Its Officials," *Hind Swaraj*, 1909

Historically, revolution has involved two steps: tearing down and building up. Few revolutions, however, get beyond the first step and therefore produce mostly violence, misrule, and even anarchy. To successfully end the British Raj, Britain's long imperial rule over India, Gandhi proposed nothing short of revolution. However, he also proposed lifting revolution from its typically tragic historical shortcomings by declining to complete step one. Rejecting the assumption that creating change necessarily requires destroying what already is, he called for his followers to resist altogether the urge to tear down. Instead, he advocated learning from everyone and everything that may have something useful to offer.

Whereas most proponents of Indian independence proclaimed themselves "tired" of being told that India had much to learn from English political wisdom and institutions, Gandhi embraced their value. "If you are tired," he wrote, "it only betrays your impatience." Gandhi suggested that anyone who offers us valuable lessons is in the position of a parent. He explained that, as children, we do not condemn our parents because they cannot run with us. "What does it matter if he cannot run with us? A nation that is desirous of securing Home Rule"–that is, of creating truly revolutionary change–"cannot afford to despise its ancestors."

Building on what has come before and on what exists is not a refusal to depart from the methods and values of the past, but creating positive change does not oblige us to despise what has come before. The fact is that most so-called inventions may be more accurately described as innovations. For example, the creators of the integrated circuit did not despise the inventors of the transistor that preceded their work any more than those transistor engineers condemned the creators of the vacuum tube. Each innovator learned from those who had come before and, if anything, was grateful for the accomplishments of his forebears.

Our parents give us life and nurture. Without them, we children could not run as we do. That they may be unable to keep up with us does not diminish what they have done for us. By the same token, their inability to keep up with us does not prevent us from running. Building higher and better does not require tearing down all existing structures, but those structures must not be allowed to prevent our building higher and better. Build on what you have, Gandhi insisted. But by all means build.

■

Lesson 84

ACCEPT THE NECESSITY OF PROCESS

"Nature has not provided any way whereby we may reach a
desired goal all of a sudden."

~ "Machinery," *Hind Swaraj*, 1909

As a man of principle, Gandhi frequently found himself on the
receiving end of would-be "gotcha" critics. For example, he expressed
the belief that India would be better off without machinery because
machinery tended to multiply man's wants, create artificial needs, and
enslave what was a primarily agricultural nation both to the machines
themselves and to the industrialized nations that made and exported
the machines. Gandhi's counsel, which was to avoid machinery as
one would avoid any evil, was countered by the clever argument that
Gandhi's very words were transmitted through machinery: the
printing press. The point of this criticism was to expose the apparent
hypocrisy of his position on machinery. However, Gandhi responded
by observing that the printing press was "one of those instances which
demonstrates that sometimes poison is used to kill poison." He saw
no hypocrisy or self-contradiction in using the mechanical printing
press to help bring about the end of India's reliance on machinery.
Meaningful change on a large scale is not instantaneous, Gandhi felt,
but rather a protracted process. Doing away with machinery would
be of necessity gradual, coming about only as more and more Indians
learned to regard it as an evil.

Gandhi proposed to conduct his campaign against machinery,
not by attacking the mechanisms themselves, but by acting to
remove the need and desire for them. This would be achieved
through a process of persuasion involving every means of communication, including the printing press. When machines finally do
vanish, Gandhi explained, it will have come about because the
people decided that they are an evil. The printing press, though a
machine, will be necessary to bring about the most meaningful,

enduring, and productive change possible—change created through internal processes within human beings, not through coercion or even relatively peaceful decrees imposed from the outside. For the modern CEO, of course, the goal is not to retreat from the "evil" of technology, but Gandhi's step backward contains a powerful lesson nonetheless: Do not attempt to impose belief and instantaneous change, but use whatever means at your disposal to create a gradual revolution in the principles and sentiments of others that will eventually bring about the desired change.

■

Sacrifice and the Servant Leader

Sympathizers with and supporters of the Bolshevik Revolution, which transformed czarist Russia into a communist state in 1917, repeatedly sought the endorsement of Mohandas Gandhi for their campaign to introduce a classless society. Gandhi never wavered in his objection to communism on the grounds that it had relied on violence to bring itself into birth, yet he praised the abolition of private property and the establishment of a system wherein property was held by the state for the common good. Even so, Gandhi never wholly embraced the leveling of society. He acknowledged both the need for leaders and the inevitability of leaders. Yet this was by no means a bow to the status quo. For his revaluation of the role of leadership was as radical as anything the Bolsheviks did. In Gandhi's revolutionary universe, leaders were servants.

Indeed, Gandhi anticipated by at least half a century the model of servant leadership now widespread in the corporate and non-profit communities. As leadership guru Robert K. Greenleaf explained in his frequently quoted 1970 essay "The Servant as Leader," servant leadership "begins with the natural feeling that one wants to serve, to serve first. Then conscious choice brings one to aspire to lead." The servant-first leader "is sharply different from one who is leader first, perhaps because of the need to assuage an unusual power drive or to acquire material possessions."

If anything, the economic crisis that is ringing down the curtain on the first decade of the twenty-first century has dramatically demonstrated the need for servant leadership in government as well as the private sector. Greed as the engine of capitalism cannot sustain an enterprise for the long run. A larger view is required, one that recognizes that social justice and a generally high level of prosperity benefit everyone: every individual and every business. Producers require consumers, and a society driven by tunnel-vision rapacity cannot empower enough people with sufficient means to consume what businesses create. Servant leadership is not only ethical leadership. It is a necessary driver of sustainable capitalism.

■

Lesson 85
LEAD TALENT

"The individual has no right to live unto himself."
~ "Removal of Untouchability," *History of the Satyagraha Ashram*,
July 11, 1932

Self-satisfaction cannot be achieved by satisfying yourself. "Talents of all kinds are a trust," Gandhi wrote, "and must be utilized for the benefit of society. . . . We fully live unto ourselves when we live unto society." The great virtue of any worthwhile enterprise is the opportunity it provides each of its members to achieve self-satisfaction by creating a benefit for the entire organization. All human beings have a drive to be useful. This urge or imperative may be misplaced or sometimes obscured by other motives, but the need to be useful is there nonetheless. All that is required is the presence of the right context, the appropriate enterprise, to coax this drive to surface and make itself known. As a business leader, you can provide the context, the environment that allows, encourages, and even demands that each and all use their talents for the benefit of all. When you acknowledge, praise, and reward an individual's demonstration of skill, judgment, insight, or excellence, always do so with reference to the enterprise. Not *You are so talented!* but *That was great. We all rely on your talent. Keep it coming!*

■

Lesson 86
BE A GOOD STEWARD

"He ever gives, never wants service."

~ "A True Congressman," *Young India*, November 19, 1925

The Indian National Congress was founded in 1885, long before the Gandhi era, to promote a greater degree of native Indian governance for India. Under Gandhi's influence, the Congress became a more truly representative body, which worked toward home rule for India and, ultimately, independence. Gandhi was not a naive man. He understood that many who seek or hold political office too often do so for personal gain and fame rather than from motives of selfless service. This knowledge did not discourage him from defining a "true Congressman," and his definition can also serve to describe the true CEO, the effective corporate steward:

> A true Congressman is a true servant. He ever gives, never wants service. He is easily satisfied so long as his own comfort is concerned. He is always content to take a back seat. He is never communal or provincial. His country is his paramount consideration.

If it was a tall order, this definition was nevertheless the only pos-sible definition of an effective leader. Only a faithful servant can be a true leader. This does not mean that a true leader is a follower. He *is* unmistakably a leader—the ultimate architect and arbiter of policy and direction. But this leadership is always in the service of the enterprise, which is a body of people organized for a common pur-pose. It is the leader's job to see beyond his personal needs in order to serve the needs of the organization of which he is a part. The good steward must also see beyond his own organization, so that he understands how it relates to the industry and the community.

Just as true leadership is service, so true service is leadership. The servant leader may always render and never require service, but, in fact, by giving service, he receives the great benefit of cre-ating, guiding, and nurturing an enterprise that serves all whom it touches, including, of course, himself. What he gives is returned to him and the organization in a far greater and more valuable form.

■

Lesson 87
ENCOURAGE A RISING TIDE

> "Pure service of one's neighbours can never, from its very nature, result in disservice to those who are remotely situated."
>
> ~ "The Law of Swadeshi," *Young India,* June 18, 1931

If you think that business is of necessity a zero-sum game—that for one to win another must lose—you may find it impossible to believe that the policies you create for your organization may also benefit those outside of your organization, including your competitors. Gandhi, however, embraced the maxim, "As with the individual so with the universe" as an "unfailing principle which we would do well to lay to heart." Improve the local situation, he insisted, and you will provide a universal benefit, if only by example. Act ethically, and you may find that you have become an ambassador for your entire industry. (Conversely, cheat someone, and you may give all your colleagues a bad name.)

Leading your organization well, serving it as a good steward, can only benefit you, your enterprise, and the world beyond. Do business more effectively, more ethically, and in ways that create and enhance customer satisfaction, and you gain success for yourself as well as for your colleagues. A rising tide floats all boats, the old saying goes. Gandhi would have understood and subscribed to its message.

■

Lesson 88
RETHINK EXECUTIVE COMPENSATION

> "The man who takes for himself only enough to satisfy the needs customary in his society and spends the rest for social service becomes a trustee."
>
> ~ Answers to questions at Gandhi Seva Sangh meeting, May 6, 1939

"Greed is good."

The words put into the mouth of Gordon Gecko, the fact based fictional tycoon played by Michael Douglas in Oliver Stone's 1987 film *Wall Street*, echo very loudly as the first decade of the twenty-first century comes to a close. A year before the movie was released, Ivan Boesky, perhaps the most notorious Wall Street manipulator of his time, assured the graduating class of the School of Business Administration at the University of California, Berkeley, that "Greed is all right. . . . I think greed is healthy. You can be greedy and still feel good about yourself."

But what about the way everybody else feels about you?

What is a CEO's "just" compensation?

Gandhi had a straightforward answer: Take only what is necessary to satisfy the needs customary in your society, then spend the rest for social service, thereby becoming a trustee of the common good. Of course, a great deal depends on how one defines "necessary" and "customary." In today's society, satisfying even just these needs can be very expensive. (Gandhi's response to this reality would doubtless be to change society.) And then we must also ask whether "justice" should even enter into the matter of executive compensation. Perhaps what is "just," in our capitalistic society, is whatever you can get others to give you. (Again, Gandhi would turn to the larger picture and work toward changing that.)

These questions must be asked here, if only because, these days, a lot of people are asking them, mainly people who have neither a six-figure salary nor a golden parachute that, with complete indifference, rewards failure as it does success. The questions cannot be answered here, except, perhaps, to suggest that Gandhi's formula— "The man who takes for himself only enough to satisfy the needs customary in his society and spends the rest for social service becomes a trustee"—is the place from which an answer may begin.

■

Lesson 89
PICK YOUR FIGHTS, AND PICK THEM WISELY

> "Those who fight may expect to be injured."
> ~ "The Condition of India (continued): The Hindus & the
> Mohomedans," *Hind Swaraj*, 1909

Many business leaders relish combat. They will fight their competition in the courts and in the marketplace. They claim to understand the risks of a roll-up-your-sleeves brawl, but they almost always make the mistake of believing that the risks are strictly limited to losing. They take for granted that if you win a fight, you can only gain.

Gandhi recognized this view as inherently untrue. "Those who fight may expect to be injured," he wrote, whether you prevail or are defeated. The cost of battle, whether the result is victory or defeat, is some degree of injury. For this reason, it benefits all parties involved in a dispute to find a mutually satisfactory, mutually rewarding solution. Combat is almost never a winner-take-all proposition. Enter a fight, and you cannot be sure that you will win or lose, but you can be virtually certain that you will suffer some injury—in lost time, squandered funds, or missed opportunities. Bring lawyers into the melee, and you are likely to discover (as Gandhi, himself a lawyer, well knew) that "lawyers . . . as a rule advance quarrels instead of repressing them." If they fail to do this, "they will be considered to have degraded their profession."

Battles must be chosen with the same care as that devoted to choosing anything costly. Squandering your treasure and your time on a cheap battle is no way to lead your enterprise to prosperity or to assert yourself as an effective CEO. Before you embark on a dispute, consider that, win or lose, you will incur costs. Fighting of any kind is a purchase. Make sure the merchandise is something you really want—that is, something that will generate profit rather than incur liability—and be even more certain that you can afford the price of victory as well as defeat. Think of this not as a moral or ethical question, but one of bottom-line profitability and long term sustainability.

■

Lesson 90
LIVE YOUR VALUES

> "Everybody admits that sacrifice of self is infinitely superior to sacrifice of others."
>
> ~ "Passive Resistance," *Hind Swaraj*, 1909

In our business and financial world, which has been widely discredited for rapacious and reckless greed, the ideal of the servant leader has emerged as an ideal of entrepreneurial and corporate governance, as valued as it is elusive. Called by Gandhi passive resistance, love-force, or soul-force, it is a form of leadership that secures "rights by personal suffering." As such, "it is the reverse of resistance by arms." To compel the government to repeal an unjust law, for example, you can use "body-force"—violence—or "soul-force," which "involves sacrifice of self." In the case of protest against a bad law, Gandhi advised refusing to obey it and enduring the legal penalty for such disobedience. This was less an act of breaking the law than of declaring one's intention to have "nothing to do with" the law.

Laws, Gandhi explained, are the works of particular governments and particular men. There is nothing sacred about them. Laws that contribute to the common good should be obeyed in service to one's community, country, and fellow beings; however, unjust laws should be disavowed. "If among a band of robbers a knowledge of robbing is obligatory," Gandhi wrote, "is a pious man to accept the obligation?"

Obedience is not in itself an ethical act. Choosing to obey just laws while rejecting those that are unjust is the essence of ethical behavior. Such choices often require a high order of courage, for the lawmakers have the force of punishment in their grasp. Moreover, it is one thing to be willing to endure the consequences of disobedience personally, but quite another to lead others to do the same. The servant leader sacrifices himself and only himself. If his example of sacrifice inspires sacrifice in others, so be it: A social movement is born. But such sacrifice must not be imposed. Servant leaders foster personal responsibility in those they lead for the very reason that they do not impose their values on others. Instead, they present themselves as exemplars of the values. Servant leadership is leadership through the encouragement of emulation.

Apart from the ethical value of servant leadership, there is the organizational strength that comes when all stakeholders in an enterprise take personal responsibility for the enterprise. An organization whose members share no values, whose unity has been merely imposed on them, is far weaker and less effective than an organization in which the common values of the constituents are deeply held by each individual. In such an organization, the leader functions as a mentor who teaches by example. He begins by taking sole responsibility for his values and actions, but he also offers them as models for emulation. It is the task of such a servant leader to make the offerings so compelling, so persuasive that the members of his enterprise will accept them voluntarily and eagerly and never out of fear of suffering some penalty should they reject them.

A creative, productive enterprise requires individually creative, productive people who routinely contribute their individuality to achieve common goals, yet do not yield their individual responsibility. The only viable leadership path for such an organization is that of noncoercive example.

■

13

Suasion in Persuasion

The word *suasion* is used far less frequently these days than *persuasion*, the word of which it is the root. The latter term encompasses a wide array of coaxing measures, from massive wartime propaganda campaigns to modest advertisements used to prompt a shopper to buy two cans of diced tomatoes instead of just one. Suasion, however, implies persuasion with a specifically moral force. Gandhi's lifelong project was to insert morality—defined as the promotion of liberty, justice, and the general welfare into every act a person was persuaded to commit and every project one was persuaded to undertake. He dedicated his life to putting suasion in all persuasion.

The ethical conduct of business requires that everything the enterprise undertakes benefit all of the firm's stakeholders—including employees, stockholders, and customers—as well as the larger community. Too many CEOs think of ethics as a bonus in business, something extra the organization takes on *after* the essentials of profit and loss have been attended to. In fact, ethical business is sustainable business—business that delivers value for value received, business founded on essential truth as opposed to

essential fraud. In this chapter, we look at lessons in ethical persuasion for organizing, motivating, and sustaining collaborative effort.
The lessons apply to any enterprise, from a three-person company
to an entire nation.

■

Lesson 91
RECRUIT VOLUNTEERS

"Moreover, what I disapprove of is an organization based on force
which a State is. Voluntary organization there must be."
~Interview with Nirmal Kumar Bose, November 9–10, 1934

A company is, in principle, a voluntary organization. People join;
they are not drafted. And yet many companies are run according to
rigid organizational rules that force the individual employee to fit
the position rather than allow even a miniscule degree of latitude by
which an employee might shape the job to better suit his style, apti-
tude, experience, and talent. Most managers speak of finding a
"good fit" between employee and job, but what they really mean is
finding an employee who will allow himself to be crammed into the
job, regardless of any pinching and chafing. Square peg? Round
hole? Their first thought is to knock the corners off the peg and
leave the hole alone.

Every organization has certain functions that must be performed.
We cannot invent unnecessary positions or leave needed jobs
undone. But within these restrictions there is generally room for an
employee to find her own ways of working. In a truly voluntary
organization, this should be encouraged. To the extent that a worker
makes a job her own, she takes ownership of the results and therefore becomes that much more committed to creating excellence.

Gandhi believed that "every man is born in the world with certain natural tendencies" as well as "certain definite limitations which

he cannot overcome." He saw the organizing principle of society as making a fit between different people and the different jobs society needs done. No one should be expected to force a self-transformation—to deny natural tendencies on the one hand and ignore natural limitations on the other—in order to fit into rigidly structured positions. Yet society cannot always afford to radically alter every necessary task or leave vital roles without anyone to play them. Instead, viable social organization requires meeting in the middle: each person allowed to gravitate toward his natural calling, and each calling sufficiently flexible to become the productive property of the person who pursues it. This is the essence of voluntary organization.

As with many principles that require thought and imagination, creating a voluntary organization takes more time upfront than simply forcing people into rigidly prepared slots. In the long run, however, the upfront investment required to create the voluntary organization pays dividends in efficiency, a superior work product, greater and more useful innovation, and increased employee commitment. The latter is vitally important, since the costs of employee turnover are considerable. By compromising organizational rigidity, you may avoid unnecessary expense as well as undesirable compromises in a host of other areas, which makes for a leaner and a more consistently competitive company.

■

Lesson 92
COMPETITION REQUIRES A COMPETITOR

"We have to be thankful to Lord Curzon."

~ "The Partition of Bengal," *Hind Swaraj*, 1909

In 1905, George Curzon—1st Marquess Curzon of Kedleston, His Majesty's viceroy of India—partitioned Bengal into two separate provinces, mainly for the convenience of imperial administration and without any regard for the Bengalese. When those people tried to reason with Curzon, "in the pride of power he disregarded all their prayers. He took it for granted that Indians could only prattle, that they could never take any effective steps. He used insulting language, and in the teeth of all opposition partitioned Bengal." The day of the partition, Gandhi argued, was the day India awoke to the injustice of Britain's power over India. In this act of oppression, India's dream of independence was born. "The shock the British power received through the Partition has never been equaled by any other act." This exercise of British power, because it was so visibly and dramatically unjust, was self-destructive—the beginning of the end of British power in India.

Gandhi did not hate Lord Curzon. On the contrary, he was thankful to him, for it was his tyranny that awakened India to the possibility of liberty. Gandhi well understood that resistance requires something to resist.

Even if you and your company have broken through to create a genuinely unique product or a service that no one else offers, your monopoly is not likely to last—and the more successful you are, the more quickly you will be joined by competitors. The CEO who merely bemoans the existence of competitors in a crowded market deserves the failure to which he dooms his enterprise. An effective business leader, on the other hand, is always thankful for competitors because their existence makes his enterprise competitive.

■

Lesson 93
AIM FOR THE HEART

> "But non-violence, which is a quality of the heart, cannot come by
> an appeal to the brain."
>
> ~ "Both Happy and Unhappy," *Harijan,* June 29, 1940

The really important values—such as, for Gandhi, nonviolence—reside in the heart rather than the head. Gandhi declared that non-violence could not be adopted as a "mere policy," but had to be a "creed" or "passion," and he pointed out that a "man with a passion expresses it in every little act of his."

Too often, today's business leaders are embarrassed by heart and passion. Their approach to business is intellectual and strictly by the book. To be sure, operating exclusively by instinct and emotion is not a sustainable leadership philosophy, but to discount emotion, feeling, heart, and passion is to sever yourself and your organization from an incalculable source of energy. One of Gandhi's favorite American writers, Ralph Waldo Emerson, wrote that "nothing great is ever accomplished without enthusiasm." Why lead in a manner that shuts the door on the possibility of greatness? Recognize with Gandhi the power of passion. Joined to intelligence, it can drive the highest excellence.

∎

Lesson 94

UNDERSTANDING IS OPTIONAL

> "I know that a whole people can adopt [nonviolence] without
> accepting it as its creed and without understanding its philosophy.
> People generally do not understand the philosophy of all their
> acts."
>
> ~ "Independence vs. Swaraj," *Young India,* January 12, 1928

Enlightened leaders of all sorts of organizations take for granted the importance of ensuring that everyone in the enterprise acquires a thorough understanding of the principles by which the organization operates, including not only the "what" and the "how" of the operation, but the "why." The need of such knowledge throughout the organization seems virtually self-evident, which is why Gandhi's observation that a whole people can adopt a principle without necessarily embracing it as a creed or even understanding its philosophy is downright stunning.

Just what is the implication of this statement?

Surely it is not a call to ignorance. Gandhi, after all, took great pains to explain himself, to detail the rationale of his policies, tactics, and strategies. He offered enlightenment to all who cared to read his words, but he also realized that a truly compelling policy, tactic, or strategy needs no justification or explanation. If it is right and valuable, the idea will be embraced, as it were, instinctively. We may adopt this as a kind of "smell test" by which a proposed course of action can be evaluated. If something *smells* right, chances are it is right. If, however, it feels wrong, you can probably assume that it is wrong.

A corollary to the smell test is the following rule of thumb: If a proposed course of action requires elaborate rationalization, there is probably something wrong with it. Ethical and ethically profitable ideas are generally capable of the most elegantly simple presentation, whereas ethically dubious ideas usually call for long-winded exercises in tortured logic. Contrast, say, the Declaration of

Independence with such U.S. Supreme Court decisions as that in
the Dred Scott Case (1857), which justified slavery, or *Plessy v.
Ferguson* (1896), which rationalized racial segregation, or *Bush v. Gore*
(2000), which decided the contested outcome of a presidential elec-
tion on a transparently partisan and corrupt basis. All of these decisions required long and tedious explanations that are both painful
to read and difficult to untangle.

Willful ignorance is never preferable to understanding.
However, understanding is no guarantee of a good decision, and
the simple appeal of conscience should never be discounted, let
alone ignored. Ethical decisions require no fine print.

■

Lesson 95
MARRY INTELLECT TO EMOTION

> "You are at the mercy of the mob. So long as there is sympathy
> between you and the mob, everything goes well. Immediately the
> cord is broken, there is horror."
>
> ~ "Democracy vs. Mobocracy," *Young India*, September 8, 1920

As a popular leader, Gandhi was always at pains to avoid becoming
a demagogue whose words would create not a purposefully organized movement but a mob. In addition to the obvious dangers of
mob action—injury, property destruction, and even death—there is
immediate danger to the would-be leader who is, in the case of mob
action, nothing more than an instigator. He may receive great adula-
tion from the mob, but this is not the same as devotion to the cause
he represents. It is an entirely personal and emotional relationship.
As such, if the "sympathy" between the mob and the leader should
suddenly snap, "there is horror."

Beware of appealing to raw emotion. A roused body of people
packs the energy of a wild animal, and you may find that you

have latched on to a tiger's tail. As mentioned in Lesson 93, today's business leaders, from managers to CEOs, typically shy away from delivering "inspirational" talks. This is a mistake. Your employees—human beings—are not pure intellect, so it is important to tap into the spirit and feelings of your workforce. However, the even greater mistake is to appeal exclusively to emotion. The energy this releases emerges uncontrolled and without productive direction.

Gandhi balanced his emotional appeals with a campaign of education. He sought simultaneously to energize his audiences and to provide clear direction for that energy. The ideal motivational talk marries head to heart, and the best way to do this is to present ideas, objectives, and goals that, in themselves, join together intellect and emotion. A genuinely inspiring program embodies inherently inspiring values and, therefore, readily lends itself to a motivational presentation that is both intellectually cogent and emotionally compelling. Ensure that the subject matter of your motivational message combines direction with feeling. Then put this matter into words that are clear and unadorned. Be generous with the nouns and verbs, but sparing with adjectives and adverbs. Let the compelling facts speak for themselves. If you find that the facts alone are not very compelling, then rethink your program before you present it. Inspiration should inhere in the subject and require few, if any, emotional additives.

■

Lesson 96
REHEARSE SPONTANEITY

> "Above all, everyone should obey volunteers' instructions without question."
>
> ~ "Democracy vs. Mobocracy," *Young India*, September 8, 1920

As spontaneous demonstrations grew in size and volume during the campaign for Indian home rule, Gandhi became increasingly wary of mob violence and was even more concerned about the kinds of accidents often associated with large, unregulated crowds. When it occurred to him that spontaneity could be disciplined and controlled, he drew up a list of rules for the guidance of the volunteers responsible for policing the crowds that greeted movement activists at train stations. Some of the rules included:

- There should be no raw volunteers accepted for big demonstrations. Therefore none but the most experienced should be at the head.

- At stations, volunteers should not all be centred at one point, namely, where the reception committee should be. But they should be posted at different points in the crowd.

- Large crowds should never enter the station. They cannot but inconvenience traffic. There is as much honour in staying out as in entering the station.

- At meetings volunteers should be dispersed among the crowd. They should learn flag and whistle signalling in order to pass instructions from one to another when it is impossible for the voice to carry.

- It is no part of the audience to preserve order. They do so by keeping motionless and silent.

The most telling rule concerned "national cries"—shouts of nationalist slogans. These, Gandhi advised, "must be fixed and must be raised not anyhow, at any time or all the time, but just on the arrival of the train, on the heroes [activists] reaching the coach and on the route at fair intervals." He continued:

> No objections need be raised to this on the score of the demonstration becoming mechanical and not spontaneous. The spontaneity will depend upon numbers, the response to the cries, above all the general look of the demonstrators, not the greatest number of noises or the loudest. It is the training that a nation receives which characterizes the nature of its demonstrations. A Mohammedan silently worshipping in his mosque is no less demonstrative that a Hindu temple-goer making a noise either through his voice or his gong or both.

Mass emotion, as Gandhi saw it, did not require being given free vent in wild, chaotic demonstrations, which savored of mobocracy instead of true democracy. In an effective mass demonstration—a demonstration that communicated eloquently to the British authorities, the world, and the rest of India—emotion certainly needed to be manifested, but so did a natural, unforced orderliness and dignity. The enthusiasm had to be channeled. In effect, the spontaneity needed to be regulated and rehearsed. To those who contended that such demonstrations are contrived and insincere, Gandhi responded to the effect that everything important about spontaneity was contained within the sincerity of the peoples' beliefs. No one can deny that a gifted orator can express sincere passion through words; no one would judge a passionate speech to be less dignified than an inarticulate cry. The difference is that speech is the product of disciplined emotion, whereas a shout is the sound of emotion dished up raw.

Where issues of motivation are concerned, it is always risky to rely on spontaneity. Inspire the people of your organization by rehearsing your own spontaneity. There is nothing wrong with injecting great passion into what you say, but there is no rule dictating that passionate expression must be absolutely off-the-cuff and impulsive. Prepare for its expression with as much serious thought as Gandhi devoted to preparing for and regulating "spontaneous" demonstrations, and you will multiply the motivational force of enthusiastic speech without risking a garbled message or a message you did not intend to convey.

■

Lesson 97
RETALIATE? NO, *EDUCATE*

"Ignorance is no provocation."

– "Non-violence," *Young India,* March 9, 1922

Historically, most revolutions became retaliations and therefore failed to bring the benefits they promised. Gandhi's great innovation in conducting revolutionary change was to regard the powers that be, in so far as they do wrong, to be suffering from ignorance, not evil intentions. The appropriate response to ignorance is education, not retaliation. Gandhi set out to educate the British overlords and the people of India alike. In the process, he hoped to educate the world.

A CEO is empowered to give orders. Doing so is without doubt an executive function, but it is not leadership. Whereas an executive issues an order, a leader exercises intellectually and emotionally compelling reason, not because he is less powerful than an executive but because he wants to elicit intelligent collaboration rather than thoughtless obedience. The most potent form of such persuasion is education. Present the facts—the what, why, and how—clearly and compellingly, and you get people to think for themselves. The value of thinking for oneself is obvious—nothing is more persuasive than one's own thoughts.

Education works on employees and opponents alike. It converts the uncooperative into a collaborator and the nonbeliever into one of the faithful. Education is explanation and advocacy, with the emphasis on explanation. Present the facts compellingly, and the presentation itself will provide sufficient advocacy to make your case. If you find it impossible to present a compelling case based solely on the facts, it is time to reassess the facts and reevaluate the wisdom of whatever course of action you contemplate. This, too, is education, and we all need it.

■

Truth

This final chapter offers three lessons based on the single word Gandhi himself chose to describe the object of his life's work: truth.

■

Lesson 98
ASK THE QUESTION OF TRUTH

> "The only motive is . . . to find out the Truth, and to follow it."
> ~Preface, *Hind Swaraj*, 1909

Few of us would admit to rejecting the truth, and fewer still would claim that such rejection is desirable. Yet it is quite probable that some of the time—perhaps much of the time—we do turn our backs on the truth for the simple reason that we don't do the hard work of finding it. When we take a job, or even embark on a career, we typically take a great deal for granted. We rarely examine the assumptions on which a job, a profession, a career, a project, or an enterprise is founded. We walk into the building, which is already built, and we do not think to examine its foundation.

Gandhi was born into a nation effectively owned by another nation. Remarkably few, either in India or in Britain, questioned this reality. Gandhi, however, refused simply to accept it. He did not reflexively reject it, either, but instead examined it on the basis of this question: *Was the relation of India to Great Britain founded on truth?* It was a basic question, and precisely because it was so basic, few ever thought to ask it. There were many who questioned whether the relation between the two countries was "just" or "desirable" or "intolerable," but Gandhi pushed these questions aside as subordinate to the only question that really mattered: *Was the relation truthful?* Unless this could be answered in one word—yes—it had to be answered with another single, simple, unambiguous word: no. And from this answer he could derive a course of action as well as its justification.

Bear in mind that, for Gandhi, *truthful* was no mere synonym for *factual*. Rather, it described a relation, an activity, or the product of an activity that offered fair value—equal benefit and full justice—to everyone partaking of it or affected by it. Anything other than fair value was false. As Gandhi understood, all worthwhile activity—all genuinely profitable, sustainable enterprise—depends on the ability to answer the question, *Is this truthful?* It is the first and last question any CEO must ask.

Yet many never ask it. The collapse of major banks and venerable securities firms beginning in 2008 flowed from the failure of corporate leaders to question the truth of their firms' investments—in other words, to examine the basis in real value of securities backed by loans and mortgages whose worth ranged from dubious to fraudulent. Likewise, the *apparently* sudden collapse of the American auto industry may be traced to decades of avoiding questions of truth. Generations of automobile CEOs turned their backs on issues of energy cost and availability, of environmental impact, and of basic quality and fair value. Sudden? As early as the 1920s, General Motors president Alfred P. Sloan Jr. articulated for his company and his industry the doctrine of "planned obsolescence," the policy of introducing minor cosmetic changes to car offerings every year while holding engineering improvements to a three-year cycle at best. The objective was to make consumers dissatisfied with their purchase within a year so that they would be motivated to buy a new car, with which they were also destined to become dissatisfied in another twelve months. The demanding pace of cosmetic innovation overshadowed the drive toward innovation in basic engineering. Indeed, durability and enduring value were regarded as inimical to achieving high yearly sales. (Truly satisfied customers do not believe they need a new car every year.) For a time, planned obsolescence produced a prosperous industry, but also created one that was doomed to eclipse by foreign manufacturers who seriously questioned the truth of their products and derived answers that compelled them to focus on excellence in engineering and the delivery of enduring value rather than mere alterations to sheet metal.

Lesson 99
DEMAND TRUTH

> "Satyagraha literally means insistence on truth. This insistence
> arms the votary with matchless power."
> ~ "Some Rules of Satyagraha," *Young India*, February 27, 1930

For Gandhi, *satyagraha* meant the insistence on truth. This concept can aid any leader in maintaining focus on what really matters: on objectives and goals, rather than on distractions that involve personality conflicts and puffed-up egos. Consider Gandhi's first rule for a "satyagrahi, i.e., a civil resister." He or she "will harbor no anger." Then ponder the second rule, which obliges the satyagrahi to "suffer the anger of the opponent" and to put up (rule number three) "with assaults from the opponent" without retaliation, but never submitting "out of fear of punishment or the like, to any order given in anger."

The lesson here is always to lead toward the objectives and goals you have defined. Focus on these rather than on the emotions and egos involved. Remember that your purpose is not to defeat anyone but to achieve your objectives and goals. Toward this end, control your own negative emotions and allow the emotions that are aimed at you to wash over you without provoking a retaliatory response. Never allow anger or fear to deflect you from your course. As Gandhi pointed out in his seventh rule, "Non-retaliation excludes swearing and cursing" as well.

Gandhi's ninth rule barred a civil resister from saluting "the Union Jack" but also from "insulting it or any officials, whether English or Indian." You are not obliged to deliver empty flattery, to praise what you do not deem worthy of praise, or to give lip service to things in which you do not believe; however, no leader, no CEO, no manager should go out of the way to insult opponents, the competition, or anyone else.

Respect is the proper climate for conducting business, and neither empty flattery nor egregious insults are compatible with a climate of respect. This extends to protecting others from insult or attack. Gandhi's rule eleven called for civil resisters to protect "officials from . . . insult or attack even at the risk of his [own] life." You will almost certainly not be called on to take so grave a risk, but because insults and personal attacks are incompatible with a climate of respect, it is your duty to defend even your opponents against such things.

Gandhi's great challenge in leading a mass movement toward profound change was to rouse, raise, and maintain the passion of commitment without ever allowing emotions to obscure the purpose of the movement or to cause harm to others—an evil in itself that would also morally discredit the movement.

Lesson 100
TRUTH ALWAYS TRIUMPHS

"The strength of a warrior is not measured by reference to his weapons but by his firmness of mind."

~ "Satyagraha–Not Passive Resistance," September 2, 1917

Corporate battles are fought daily with any number of weapons, including leveraged buyouts, hostile takeovers, lawsuits, aggressive marketing, predatory or quasi-predatory business practices designed to strong-arm the competition, corporate espionage, aggressive price cutting, and on and on. Many of these aggressive practices are effective in the short term, which, often, is all that is really required. But over the long term, it is the character of a company that sustains it. Victories won by the various weapons in the arsenal of business tend to be transitory, giving rise to new fights, whereas the self-image and self-identity of a firm endures for as long as the leadership and constituents of the company are willing to live up to established core principles.

Ethics is certainly a part of this corporate "firmness of mind," but so are other values, such as commitment to excellence, to service, to creating customer satisfaction, and to developing and rewarding talent. It is not wrong to use every legal weapon at your disposal, but it is an act of self-delusion to expect long-term change from these short-term expedients. Formulating and living up to sound core values is a commitment to truth, after which, Gandhi observed, "Nothing more need be said. Truth alone triumphs. . . . Truth always wins."

■

A Gandhi Chronology

1619

First British outpost established in India.

1858

Commencement of the British Raj (British colonial rule).

1869

Born at Porbandar, Kathiawar, India.

1876

Betrothed to Kasturba Makanji.

1883

Married to Kasturba.

1888

Goes to London to study law.

1892

Returns to India and begins law practice.

1893

Moves to South Africa as lawyer for an Indian firm; first experience of racial discrimination.

1894

Becomes Indian rights activist in South Africa.

1899

Organizes Indian Ambulance Corps in the Second (Great) Boer War.

1902

After a brief stay in India, returns to South Africa at the request of the Indian community there.

1903

Opens law office in Johannesburg; starts publication of *Indian Opinion*, a political journal.

1904

Founds Phoenix Settlement, a utopian cooperative community near Durban.

1906

Organizes the Indian Ambulance Corps during the Zulu Rebellion; organizes mass meeting to protest proposed anti-Indian immigrant legislation in South Africa's Transvaal.

1907

Launches first satyagraha campaign to protest compulsory registration of "Asians" (Indians in South Africa).

1908

Tried for his protest organizing activity; sentenced to two months' imprisonment in Johannesburg; released after conference with South African premier General Jan Smuts; wounded by an Indian extremist in an assassination attempt for compromising with Smuts; responds to Smuts's abrogation of compromise with a second satyagraha campaign, in which Indians burned their required registration certificates; arrested, tried, and imprisoned.

1909

Sails to England to plead the case of Indian persecution; writes *Hind Swaraj*.

1910

Establishes Tolstoy Farm near Johannesburg.

1913

Third satyagraha campaign begins: 2,000 to 3,000 Indians violate South African law by crossing the Transvaal border; repeatedly arrested, tried, imprisoned, then released.

1914

Compromise with Smuts results in passage of Indian Relief Act; organizes Indian Ambulance Corps in England at outbreak of World War I but, stricken with pleurisy, returns to India.

1915

Establishes Satyagraha Ashram at Kochrab, near Ahmedabad, and admits an "untouchable" family to the compound.

1917

Moves ashram to the Sabarmati River; leads campaign for rights of peasants on indigo plantations.

1918

Leads millworkers' strike at Ahmedabad and satyagraha campaign for peasant farmers in Kheda; agrees that Indians should be recruited to fight in World War I and inaugurates a recruiting campaign; recovers from a bout of serious illness and learns traditional Indian spinning.

1919

Oppressive Rowlatt Acts passed in March; Gandhi responds by organizing first nationwide nonviolent noncooperation campaign; Amritsar Massacre takes place on April 13.

1920

Elected president of All-India Home Rule League; organizes a second national satyagraha campaign.

1921

Officiates at ceremony that opens the first shop to sell homespun in Bombay (Mumbai); leads a public burning of imported English cloth; begins wearing homespun loincloth.

1922

Suspends mass civil disobedience after violence at Chauri Chaura; arrested on a charge of sedition; pleads guilty, compelling judge to reluctantly sentence him to six years' imprisonment.

1923

Writes *Satyagraha in South Africa* and begins his autobiography while in prison.

1924

Released from prison.

1929

Congress declares independence and commences boycott of the British-sanctioned Indian legislature; Gandhi launches the third all-India satyagraha campaign.

1930

Leads a 240-mile "Salt March" in defiance of British law against making salt (forcing Indians to buy imported salt); Gandhi and nearly 100,000 Indians are jailed.

1931

Released; Gandhi-Irwin Pact (which, among other concessions, removes salt restrictions) signed, whereupon Gandhi ends civil disobedience campaign; attends international conference in London; returns to India and begins fourth national satyagraha campaign.

1932

Arrested and detained without trial in Bombay (Mumbai); begins "perpetual fast unto death" in prison to protest British government's giving untouchables separate electorate; results in the Poona Pact, which gave the "depressed" class much greater legislative representation and eliminated the separate electorate.

1933

Replaces *Young India* with *Harijan*, a journal devoted to removing untouchability; disbands Sabarmati ashram; imprisoned again; begins fast against government's refusal to allow him to continue anti-untouchability campaign while in prison; falls seriously ill.

1934

Launches All-India Village Industries Association.

1936

Settles in Segaon, a village in the Central Provinces; establishes Sevagram ashram.

1939

Begins fast unto death in a renewed satyagraha campaign.

1940

Launches civil-disobedience campaign to protest government's ban against Indian expression of opinion regarding World War II; 23,000 arrested and imprisoned this year.

1942

Indian National Congress passes "Quit India" resolution, transforming home rule campaign into a campaign for outright independence; imprisoned.

1943

Fasts for twenty-one days to protest lack of progress in negotiations with viceroy.

1944

Wife Kasturba dies in prison, prompting officials to release Gandhi out of concern for his declining health; as of this final imprisonment, Gandhi had spent a total of 2,338 days behind bars during his lifetime; consults with Muslim leaders on Hindu-Muslim unity.

1946

Meets with British Cabinet Mission in New Delhi, working toward an Indian provisional government preparatory to independence; tours East Bengal in an effort to end riots over Muslim representation in the Indian provisional government.

1947

Continues campaign to reconcile Hindu and Muslim interests; embarks on New Delhi conferences with Viceroy Lord Mountbatten (representing the British Crown) and Muhammad Ali Jinnah (representing India's Muslims) in an effort to hammer out a provisional government for an independent India; Indian National Congress votes to partition India by creating the Muslim country of Pakistan; on August 14, 1947, Britain officially withdraws from India; bloody riots break out between Muslims and Hindus in Calcutta over the partition issue; Gandhi ends the violence there by commencing a new "fast unto death."

1948

Gandhi is assassinated on January 30 by a Hindu extremist, Nathuram Vinayak Godse, outraged by Gandhi's attempts to reconcile Hindus and Muslims.

1950

India ends its status as a Dominion of the Crown on January 26, proclaiming itself a republic.

1956

Pakistan renounces dominion status, proclaiming itself a republic.

1971

The Pakistani Civil War results in the secession of East Pakistan as Bangladesh.

Further Reading

Selected Writings by Gandhi

Gandhi's literary output is staggering, his *Collected Works* (New Delhi: Publications Division, n.d.) running to one hundred volumes. His major, readily obtainable books include:

Autobiography: The Story of My Experiments with Truth. New York: Dover, 1983.

Hind Swaraj and other Writings, edited by Anthony J. Parel. Cambridge, UK: Cambridge University Press, 1997.

Non-Violent Resistance (Satyagraha). Mincola, NY: Dover, 2001.

Recommended Anthologies of Works by Gandhi

The following anthologies present a generous selection of Gandhi's seminal works and thought:

Attenborough, Richard, ed. *The Words of Gandhi*. New York: Newmarket Press, 1982.

Dalton, Dennis, ed. *Mahatma Gandhi: Selected Political Writings.*
Indianapolis: Hackett, 1996.

Fischer, Louis, ed. *The Essential Gandhi: An Anthology of His Writings
on His Life, Work, and Ideas.* New York: Vintage, 1983.

Jack, Homer A. *The Gandhi Reader: A Sourcebook of His Life and
Writings.* Bloomington: Indiana University Press, 1956; reprinted,
New York: Grove Press, 1994.

Mukherjee, Rudrangshu, ed. *The Penguin Gandhi Reader.* New York:
Penguin, 1996.

Works about Gandhi and His Circle

Barr, Mary F. *Bapu: Conversations and Correspondence with Mahatma
Gandhi.* Bombay: International Book House, 1956.

Birla, G. D. *In the Shadow of the Mahatma.* Bombay: Orient
Longmans, 1953.

Bose, Nirmal K. *My Days with Gandhi.* Calcutta: Nishana, 1953.

Bourke-White, Margaret. *Halfway to Freedom.* New York: Simon and
Schuster, 1949.

Brecher, Michael. *Nehru.* London: Oxford University Press, 1959.

Brown, Judith. *Gandhi: Prisoner of Hope.* Delhi: Oxford University
Press, 1990.

Campbell-Johnson, Alan. *Mission with Mountbatten.* London: Robert
Hale, 1972.

Catlin, George. *In the Path of Mahatma Gandhi.* London: Macdonald,
1948; Chicago: Regnery, 1950.

Chatterjee, Margaret. *Gandhi's Religious Thought.* New Delhi:
Macmillan, 1983.

Datta, Dhirendra M. *The Philosophy of Mahatma Gandhi.* Madison:
University of Wisconsin Press, 1953.

Erikson, Erik. *Gandhi's Truth.* New York: Norton, 1969.

Fischer, Louis. *The Life of Mahatma Gandhi.* New York: Harper, 1950.

Gandhi, Rajmohan. *Gandhi: The Man, His People, and the Empire.* Berkeley: University of California Press, 2008.

Green, Martin. *Gandhi: Voice of a New Age Revolution.* New York: Continuum, 1993.

Huttenback, Robert A. *Gandhi in South Africa.* Ithaca, NY: Cornell University Press, 1971.

Walker, Roy. *Sword of Gold: A Life of Mahatma Gandhi.* London: Indian Independence Union, 1945.

Weber, Thomas. *On the Salt March.* New Delhi: HarperCollins, 1997.

Wolpert, Stanley. *Jinnah.* New York: Oxford University Press, 1984.

Film

Gandhi, the 1982 epic film by director Richard Attenborough and starring Ben Kingsley in the title role, is a remarkable piece of film making and an accurate, vivid representation of Gandhi's life, from his awakening to issues of social justice in South Africa through Indian independence and his assassination. Both the director and star won Academy Awards. The film is frequently shown on cable and broadcast television and is available on DVD.

Lesson Index

Lesson 71
Ask and Answer the Question of Commitment 132
He perhaps puts an emphasis on the result, whereas I put [it] on the means.

Lesson 72
Demolish the Deviation, Not the Original 134
In order to demolish this distortion let us not seek to demolish the original.

Lesson 73
Even an Idealist Must Sometimes Choose Pragmatism 135
Where there is danger from tigers, wolves and so on, then killing them becomes inevitable.

CHAPTER 10
Lesson 74
Create Genuine Relationships, Not False Labels 138
The bond of the slave is snapped the moment he considers himself to be a free being.

Lesson 75
Decline to Be a Victim 139
The English have not taken India; we have given it to them.

Lesson 76
Take Responsibility, Then Take Command 140
But I make a mistake. How can Manchester be blamed?

Lesson 77
Be Power's Steward, Not Its Slave 142
We are opposing the intoxication of power, that is, the blind application of law, and not authority as such. The difference must never be lost sight of.

Lesson 78
Exploit the Power of Dissatisfaction 143
This discontent is a very useful thing.

Index